Looking for One Smart Cookie Instead of a Zillion of 'em?

Here are 75 delicious recipes for all kinds of cookies in the practical, time-saving quantities you want: "cookies by the dozen." From all-American chocolate chip and oatmeal raisin classics to exotic international delights, such as Greek Almond, Hungarian Walnut and Sour Cream, and Chinese Almond Cookies . . . from a tempting assortment of meringues, madeleines, and shortbreads to a wide variety of holiday treats, you'll find recipes for all the greatest cookies you ever wanted to make—in the small quantities you want to make them in.

An Alternate Selection of Book-of the-Month Club's
HomeStyle® Books

COOKIES
BY THE
DOZEN

● ● ●

Over 75 Irresistible Recipes
for Just a Dozen Cookies Each

———

DOLORES KOSTELNI

WARNER BOOKS

A Time Warner Company

Warner Books, Inc., 1271 Avenue of the Americas, New York, NY 10020

A Time Warner Company

Printed in the United States of America
First Printing: October 1995

10 9 8 7 6 5 4 3 2 1

Library of Congress Cataloging-in-Publication Data

Kostelni, Dolores.
    Cookies by the dozen : over 75 irresistible recipes for just a
dozen cookies each / Dolores Kostelni.
        p.   cm.
    Includes bibliographical references and index.
    ISBN 0-446-67027-8 (trade paper)
    1. Cookies.   I. Title.
TX772.K72   1995
641.8'654—dc20   94-23890
                                        CIP

Cover illustration by David Montiel
Cover design by Julia Kushnirsky
Book design by Giorgetta Bell McRee

Acknowledgments

I thank my family for helping to make this book a reality. Your love and encouragement grace every page.

I owe a lifetime of gratitude to my parents, Marie and Hugo Surmonte, who ignited my taste buds and kept them on the right track.

Jim, my honey, you are the perfect cook's companion. Thank you for the many trips around the globe to sample and savor a world of cookies.

J. H., for your unwavering appreciation of everything chocolate.

Charles, for your lively, expert opinions, our family sage, and thoughtful oatmeal cookie connoisseur.

My twin sons, Jeff and Hugo. Jeff, the guy who sees magic in rainbows, I was thrilled you needed only a few cookies at a time to serve your guests. Thank you for sharing this idea with me. Hugo, I cherish your advice and contagious perseverance.

Natalie, fellow writer and critic-at-large, my thanks for your concern and your many evaluations of my small, sweet delights.

I am indebted to the master bakers through the centuries. They established the foundation recipes for cookies, making it easier for me to look over their shoulders and create my interpretations.

Meg Ruley, my truly special literary agent, my undying gratitude for your guidance, enthusiasm, and support.

Karen Kelly, my astute editor at Warner Books, and to her staff, most especially to Libby Kessman and Mari Okuda, my appreciation for your creativity, patience, and facile way with words. You've made my first cookbook come alive.

Contents

Overview

If there were a hall of fame for sweets, cookies would be the first elected. Cookies are noble and comforting. They refresh, restore, and give a lift. Cookies nourish nostalgia and cultivate well-being. They are a bright spot to come home to at the end of a school day. With a glass of milk, they banish all the demons of the night.

Everyone loves homemade cookies. Even folks who profess not to like sweets have a real soft spot when it comes to freshly made cookies. And making cookies brings back all sorts of good, secure feelings. Irresistible aromas perfume the house, recalling more leisurely times. It's always nice to have a few cookies on hand to share with unexpected guests and family, especially ones you've made yourself with wholesome, hand-selected ingredients.

But an unwanted avalanche occurs with standard recipes: They make too many—48, 60, 72, 96. With the making, baking, and cooling of batch after batch, they command a half day's time at the oven.

When there are only two for cookies and milk or when you want to provide an impromptu reward of freshly baked goodies, *Cookies by the Dozen* is the answer.

Cookies by the Dozen solves the age-old jillions-of-cookies puzzle. This unique cookbook offers an enticing collection of seventy-five favorite cookie recipes in the handy, timesaving quantity you want—an even dozen or, at the very most, a baker's dozen. Here, at last, is a collection of authentic and delectable cookie recipes in scaled-down proportions.

Cookies by the Dozen is lots of fun. It presents easy, quickly accomplished recipes that are mixed and baked in a few minutes. No more endless numbers of pans going in and out of the oven. Just one cookie sheet and one 8 × 8-inch pan are all you'll ever need for seventy-two of the seventy-five recipes in *Cookies by the Dozen*. And shorter baking times mean reduced energy consumption.

Equipment is basic and simple and just what you have already: A small bowl and a handheld mixer—or a wooden spoon—are all that's necessary for creating *Cookies by the Dozen*. Forget about hauling out your battery of industrial-strength appliances.

Cookies by the Dozen is convenient. All of the ingredients are usually right there in your pantry and no farther than the baking section of your favorite supermarket. With smaller yields, there are no lengthy shopping lists calling for two pounds of butter or three boxes of brown sugar. Most of the recipes call for a minimum of ingredients: only four tablespoons of butter, a third of a cup of sugar, and less than a cup of flour. Rarely is more than an egg yolk or egg white necessary for creating these beguiling delights. These recipes are designed for busy people who have little time yet who continue to savor dandy cookies they make themselves.

The recipes in *Cookies by the Dozen* embrace popular regional sweets and well-known international delights. These cookies capture a wide range of textures that are sure to please everyone. Some are soft, many chewy, some gooey, a few crunchy: All-American Chewy Chocolate Chip, World's Best Oatmeal Raisin Cookies, Surprise Macaroons, an assortment of enticing meringues, a few madeleine spin-offs, Scarlett's Kisses, The Most Chocolate Brownies (they make their own rich glaze), Lemon Crowned Shortbread, Turtle-Stuffed Oatmeal Shortbread, Citrus Wafers, Cowboy Cookies, plus some of the South's sweetest secrets—preachers and Delta Bars—in never before, unforgettable, original variations as well as many of the author's own personal recipes, her family's tried and true favorites.

Cookies by the Dozen is also practical. Not only can you bake a different kind each night of the week without having leftovers for the neighborhood, but you'll also delight in the harvest of special seasonal cookies, like Glazed Pumpkin Pillows, Christmas Stars, Fruitcake Déjà Vu Cookies (unusual because they're made with already baked fruitcake), and Cranberry and Nut-Stuffed Oatmeal Shortbread (to incorporate leftover sauce from Thanksgiving). Luscious Raspberry Brownies are certain to beguile and bewitch a sweetheart on Valentine's Day. There are unbaked cookies, too, perfect sweets for making in the summer without heating up the kitchen. With all of them, invaluable step-by-step directions and suggestions for overnight storing are laid out clearly. The recipes are foolproof and the results are delicious.

Cookies by the Dozen reveals the sweet secret that helps cookies maintain that desirable round shape while baking. In many instances, this same technique helps eliminate much of the distortion that occurs in warped pans when they're in the oven.

This is the cookie book that cookie munchers of the world are waiting for. *Cookies by the Dozen* is for everyone.

Introduction

Cookies are solidly woven into my adult life. They were the first goodies I baked as a bride, simply because recipes yielded a great number. Not only were there plenty for the two of us but the overflow paved a wonderfully sweet trail of introductions for me around our new neighborhood.

When our five children were young, cookies furnished hours of amusement in the mixing, cutting, and fashioning of edible crafts. And they were good to eat, too.

High Fives, actually hand cookies—they traced their own hands on sugar cookie dough and then decorated them with sprinkles and baked baubles—delivered big-time fun. So did plopping spoonfuls of drop cookies onto a baking sheet or rolling dough into cookie balls (as distinguished from meatballs) before fingerprinting them down into a patty. Making homemade cookies gave us a chance to get to know each other through easy conversation while working.

To this day, each of us enjoys particular favorites for different reasons. That's what generated the idea for *Cookies by the Dozen*. No one has the time or the desire to make trayfuls, but we all have the inclination to make a dozen cookies for ourselves and friends.

Several requirements were crucial: nothing complicated, no fancy techniques, clear recipes, exact directions, easily found supermarket ingredients, and quick, delicious results. In all instances, recipes should yield a limited number of cookies. (Unless otherwise specified, all yields are one dozen cookies.)

For several months I devised and developed, then tested and retested cookie recipes. When we got together at Thanksgiving and Christmas, those results were our holiday desserts. Taste memories were the yardstick that either passed or failed a cookie.

These recipes and directions were originally written with J.H., Charles, Jeff, Hugo, and Natalie in mind, but they're for you, too. You're invited to bake *Cookies by the Dozen* and share in some of our sweet memories.

COOKIES
BY THE
DOZEN

1

· · ·

The Basics

Cookies by the Dozen is for everyone—the novice, the experienced cook, the bachelor. It's for everyone who enjoys creating and baking wonderful cookies.

Cookies by the Dozen will help beginners master some mixing and baking techniques and terminologies because all the instructions are easy and clear. Those who already know about cookies and baking will delight in the limited quantity of cookies they will make and have on hand as well as the brief period of time it takes to make and bake them.

INGREDIENTS

Basic baking staples found in supermarkets all over the country are the ingredients for the recipes in *Cookies by the Dozen*. I've used the well-known national brands instead of regional, imported, or store labels.

Fats

Butter creates elegant flavor marriages with ingredients and produces textures that melt in your mouth. That's why I specify it in most of the recipes. Although unsalted butter is the queen of baking fats and I prefer it to salted butter, it has a short refrigerated life span. When I purchase several pounds of it at a time, I freeze most of it so its irreplaceable flavor will be fresh when I use it.

When several groups of tasters preferred the results from using solid vegetable short-ening (Crisco) or regular corn oil margarine (Fleischmann's and Mazola), I've said so in the preface to the recipes and given the reasons why. When oil is listed, I used a clear, tasteless kind, such as Crisco. Each fat gives a different result.

Flour

Unbleached all-purpose flour is my flour of choice because of its natural purity. Pillsbury and General Mills are the two brands I use interchangeably. Flour is measured from the sack or large canister by first stirring to break up the clumps, then spooning lightly into a metal dry measuring cup and leveling off with the straight edge of a table knife or pastry scraper.

Chocolate

Hershey's, Nestle's, and Baker's chocolate products are available all of the time in my area, the Shenandoah Valley of Virginia, and so I felt they would be in everyone's grocery stores, no matter what region they live in. Unsweetened baking cocoa is measured like flour and sugar by spooning into a dry measuring cup.

Sugar

When sugar is listed in a recipe it means granulated cane sugar. It is measured just like flour: Stir to break up the clumps, then spoon lightly into the cup and level with the straight edge of a table knife or pastry scraper.

A listing for brown sugar means light brown sugar that is tightly packed in the cup. This is accomplished by scooping down into the sugar and pressing it flat to pack it in the cup.

Confectioners' sugar is always specified as such and should really be sifted before measuring because it is always full of lumps that are impossible to stir or beat away. It is measured like flour and granulated sugar.

Extracts and Spices

Only pure extracts and spices from national companies were used.

Salt is used in all of the recipes. A few grains of salt plus vanilla extract go a long way in bringing out the flavor in cookies.

Measuring

This is the most important aspect of making any recipe in *Cookies by the Dozen*. Since the recipes produce only a dozen or a baker's dozen, accurate measuring is crucial to the success of every recipe. A delicate balance with the ingredients has been achieved.

Dry ingredients are measured using graduated dry measuring cups. First, stir to break up any packed clumps, then lightly spoon it to overflowing into the appropriately sized cup and level it off by scraping away the excess with the straight side of a knife or pastry scraper. Avoid exerting any downward pressure. Resist shaking the cup or packing the ingredients down unless specified as with brown sugar.

Measuring Guidelines

For consistency and success with *Cookies by the Dozen*, here are some basic guidelines for you to follow.

- Use metal dry measuring cups for dry ingredients and glass liquid cups for volume measuring of liquids.
- When measuring ⅔ cup flour or sugar, use the ⅓ cup measure twice, a total of 3½ ounces. (You might be tempted to use ½ cup plus ⅓ cup measure, which would total 4 ounces, but this would alter, if not ruin, the results.)
- A pinch is just about ⅛ teaspoon. If you have this measuring spoon, use it. Otherwise, take a pinch, what you can pick up between your index finger and thumb. If you're in doubt as to the exact amount, put the ingredient in ¼ teaspoon. If it's half, then you've got it.
- When measuring liquids, keep the cup level and steady and get down to eye level of the liquid in the cup. By looking at the liquid from an angle above or below the measurement, you get a false reading.
- Measure and cut butter neatly and evenly when it is cold. Take a look at the wrapping and see if the markings are even on both ends. If not, measure by the teaspoonful:

Three teaspoon marks equal one tablespoon. Better weigh the butter: Each stick is four ounces and go from there.

EQUIPMENT

Flat-edged aluminum cookie sheets of sturdy gauge are desirable. Cookie sheets designed like a sandwich with a layer of air in between are new on the market. No longer the exclusive item in gourmet shops, these are now in discount department stores all over the country.

If you find your cookies are burning on the bottom and you know your oven is OK, it's invariably because the pan is too thin. The "sweet secret" is to line your cookie sheets with a single or double layer of heavy-duty aluminum foil (shiny side up). The foil adds thickness, promotes even distribution of heat, decreases the potential for scorching, and increases the probability that your cookies will be uniformly shaped and won't travel all over the pan.

Most of my cookie sheets are more than ten years old, with indelible burn marks. But their greatest attribute is that they've never warped and sprung like some of my newer ones. So I prefer to always use a lining of heavy-duty aluminum foil on my cookie sheets—both old and new—because the cookies bake more evenly and don't change shape as much. Some of my newest and most expensive air-filled sheets have sprung on a corner. With a layer of heavy-duty aluminum foil, even these warped pans bake better and don't get so greatly distorted when they're in the oven.

An obvious benefit to lining the pans with foil is less cleanup. But, since I also try to be a good citizen, I wipe the foil off with a damp paper towel so it can be used again.

I wouldn't use or recommend the black baking pans because the heat distribution is difficult to control. A shiny surface brings out the best in a cookie.

An 8 × 8-inch square pan and a madeleine pan, the latter with 12 shell-shaped openings, are the other two baking pans used in *Cookies by the Dozen*. The square pan is always available everywhere, but the madeleine pan seems to appear only during the holiday seasons in department stores and kitchen shops. At any other time of year, it can be ordered from Williams-Sonoma (1-800-541-2233).

If you're out camping and all you have is a wooden spoon and a knife, it's possible to mix most of the recipes in *Cookies by the Dozen*. It's easier, though, for most of us to use a handheld mixer and a wooden spoon. They are the star performers for mixing the recipes in this book.

Whisks are handy and the ones I've found most useful measure 8 inches. For combining dry ingredients on wax paper, I like using the baby-sized 5-incher. Both are inexpensive and found in the housewares sections of supermarkets and discount stores.

Nuts can be chopped in the processor or blender, in a chopper, or by wielding a sharp, heavy chef's knife across them until the desired consistency is reached.

A very few of the recipes require pulverizing cookies or oatmeal. This can be accomplished in the food processor using the metal blade or by whirling batches of the ingredient in the blender. Of course, the rolling pin can be put to work reducing cookies to crumbs also. Just contain the cookies in a plastic bag that is covered with a kitchen towel before rolling away.

Greasing and Flouring

Because cookies are high in fat, the pans usually don't require greasing or buttering. However, the composition of some cookies requires the pans to be greased and floured. This is specified in the recipes, and in many instances, the exact technique is described for you.

Nice to Have But Not Necessary

A wooden chocolate spoon. At first glance this looks like the backside of any ordinary wooden spoon. Turn it over and discover that it lacks a bowl, making it great for mixing chocolate or any small amount of batter because there are no hiding places. Mine is made by Hugli and I found it in a kitchen shop while vacationing in Phoenix, Arizona.

Storing Cookies

Cookies happen to be terrific keepers. Even frosted or glazed cookies freeze well for up to three months; after that, the sugar breaks down and a bitterness develops.

The best method for accomplishing a good freeze is to place the cookies on a sturdy pan and flash freeze them, uncovered, until rock hard. Then pack in double freezer bags, seal, date, and label. Flash freezing prevents one from sticking to the other.

Friendly Helpfulness

Kiss unwelcome surprises good-bye by establishing an intimate, hands-on relationship with all of your appliances. I know my oven does a basically good job. However, when I'm baking cookies, I know the inside ones will not bake as quickly as the outside ones. So I place a bit less batter in the center, making the cookies on the perimeter a little larger.

Before beginning any recipe, read it through from beginning to end, visualizing the steps involved. This acts as an aid you may need to fall back on when ironing out any unfamiliar techniques.

Assemble the ingredients in the order you'll be using them. This helps to solve the mystery of "Did I add it?"

If you're melting chocolate in the microwave, be conservative and use Medium for 20 or 30 seconds. It's better to return the chocolate for additional melting after stirring a few times than it is to have seized and burned chocolate because the temperature was too high. Do the same with butter. We all know how it shoots grease missiles.

2

Cookies for Every Day and Every Reason

Drop cookies are the most fun because they're the easiest and quickest to make. Satisfaction is virtually instant. Their name derives from the way the batter drops or is pushed from the spoon into a free-form mound on a baking sheet. Some of the world's most popular cookies are the drop variety and they are whatever you want—homey, elegant, or lusciously rich.

Few cookies stir more loyalty than the All-American Chewy Chocolate Chip Cookie. You'll find its specific requirements satisfied grandly in this book: excellent definition, a high ratio of chips, and a great deal chewy with just a little crunch.

Wholesome sweets combining nutritious oatmeal with both dried and fresh fruits harmonize perfectly with today's eating awareness. Two recipes—Glazed Banana Oatmeal Mounds and World's Best Oatmeal Raisin Cookies—embrace the qualities of homespun and virtuous with richly flavored character.

Colonial Hermits, a heritage cookie from New England, has withstood the test of changing tastes during our country's 200-plus years. It marches in moist, flavor-packed step even now, with its lacing of hearty molasses and abundance of dried apples and raisins.

Everyone needs a dose of quickly made luxury. Macadamia Nut Chocolate Chip Ecstasies and Surprise Macaroons fill those requirements for something splendid.

Sensational and remarkable are the hallmarks of Potato Chip Cookies. They give new meaning to that popular snack.

All-American Chewy Chocolate Chip Cookies
Macadamia Nut Chocolate Chip Ecstasies
World's Best Oatmeal Raisin Cookies
Peanut Butter and Oatmeal Jamwiches
Miracles
Surprise Macaroons
Potato Chip Cookies
Colonial Hermits
Glazed Banana Oatmeal Mounds
Almond Gazelles
Salted Peanut Granola Cookies
Cowboy Cookies

DOLORES KOSTELNI

All-American Chewy Chocolate Chip Cookies

From coast to coast, this cookie reigns as our nation's favorite. This well-defined version boasts a soft chewiness with lots of chips studding a tasty batter. For special occasions or holidays, decorate the cookies with squiggles of melted chocolate or write your guests' names on them. This recipe makes enough for you and someone you love.

¾ cup plus 2 teaspoons all-purpose flour
¼ teaspoon baking soda
Pinch of salt
4 tablespoons (½ stick) plus 1 teaspoon unsalted butter, softened
¼ cup granulated sugar
¼ cup packed light brown sugar
1 large egg yolk
1 teaspoon vanilla extract
¼ to ½ teaspoon water
½ cup plus 3 tablespoons semisweet chocolate chips

1. With the rack positioned at the highest level, preheat the oven to 400°F.

2. Combine the flour, baking soda, and salt and set aside.

3. With the mixer on low speed, combine the butter with both sugars, the egg yolk, vanilla, and water. (The smaller quantity of water makes a puffier cookie.) Increase the speed to high and beat until thoroughly mixed and light.

4. With a spoon or dinner fork, combine the creamed mixture with the dry ingredients. (The batter appears crumbly, but as you combine the remaining ingredients, it will come together and clean the bowl.) Stir or hand knead in the chocolate chips.

5. Using a heaping tablespoonful of batter as a guide, make 13 evenly sized balls and place 2 inches apart onto a cookie sheet. Alternatively, using the tip of another spoon, push the batter by heaping tablespoonfuls onto a cookie sheet in well-spaced rounded mounds.

6. Decrease the oven temperature to 350°F. Bake the cookies 5 minutes, then reverse the pan so the back is in the front. Increase the oven temperature to 375°F. and bake 4 to 5 minutes longer. The cookies appear golden brown with small pale centers. Cookies will complete cooking as they cool on the pan. The shorter baking time produces a chewier cookie.

7. Cool cookies in the pan on a wire rack for 2 minutes. Remove the cookies to a wire rack for complete cooling.

8. If there are ever any leftover cookies, a well-sealed plastic bag or an airtight container at cool room temperature will keep them at their chewy best for overnight storage.

YIELD: *a baker's dozen*

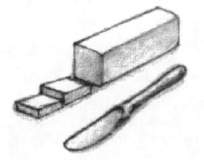

Macadamia Nut Chocolate Chip Ecstasies

The combination of macadamia nuts and chocolate chips produces this luxurious cookie. Macadamia nuts come lightly salted. If you feel you need to remove the seasoning, rub the nuts lightly with a terry cloth towel.

¾ cup plus 1 teaspoon all-purpose flour
¼ teaspoon baking soda
Pinch of salt
4 tablespoons (½ stick) plus 2 teaspoons unsalted butter, softened
¼ cup packed light brown sugar
2 tablespoons granulated sugar
1 large egg yolk
½ teaspoon vanilla extract
½ teaspoon water
½ cup plus 1 tablespoon semisweet chocolate chips
⅓ cup coarsely chopped lightly salted macadamia nuts

1. With the rack positioned at the highest level, preheat the oven to 400°F.

2. Combine the flour, baking soda, and salt and set aside.

3. In a small bowl, cream the butter with the sugars, egg yolk, vanilla, and water until fluffy and light.

4. With a spoon or fork, stir in the dry ingredients. (The mixture appears dry and crumbly, but as you combine the remaining ingredients, it will come together and clean the bowl.) Fold and stir in the chocolate chips and macadamia nuts so they are distributed evenly.

5. Drop by heaping tablespoonfuls in well-spaced mounds on a cookie sheet. Alternatively, using the tip of another spoon, push the batter by heaping tablespoonfuls onto a cookie sheet in well-spaced rounded mounds. Reduce the oven temperature to 375°F.

6. Bake 5 minutes. Reverse the pan so the back is in the front and bake 3 to 5 minutes longer. The cookies continue to bake as they cool. A shorter baking time produces a soft, nicely chewy cookie, while longer baking makes a chewy cookie with crispy edges. I prefer to bake mine just under 9 minutes.

7. Cool the cookies in the pan on a wire rack 4 minutes. Remove the cookies to a wire rack for complete cooling.

8. Store any leftover cookies in an airtight container at cool room temperature.

*YIELD: **a baker's dozen***

World's Best Oatmeal Raisin Cookies

I guarantee these gently sweet and softly chewy cookies will disappear before your eyes. One of my favorite ways with these is to whirl the dry ingredients in the workbowl of the food processor. This not only combines everything but also pulverizes the oatmeal so the cookies are even more delightfully chewy.

½ cup plus 1 tablespoon all-purpose flour
¼ teaspoon baking soda
Pinch of salt
½ teaspoon ground cinnamon

⚡ ⚡ ⚡

⅔ cup plus 2 tablespoons quick-cooking oatmeal
4 tablespoons (½ stick) unsalted butter, softened
¼ cup granulated sugar
¼ cup packed light brown sugar
1 large egg white
½ teaspoon vanilla extract
½ teaspoon milk or water
⅓ cup soft currants or raisins

1. With the rack positioned at the highest level, preheat the oven to 350°F.

2. Combine the flour, baking soda, salt, cinnamon, and oatmeal and set aside.

3. In a small bowl, cream the butter with both sugars until light.

4. Beat in the egg white, vanilla, and milk or water until thoroughly mixed and creamy.

5. Using a wooden spoon or fork, combine the creamed mixture with the dry ingredients. Stir and fold in the currants or raisins until they are completely and evenly distributed.

6. Drop by generous tablespoonfuls onto a cookie sheet in 13 well-spaced mounds. Using the back of a wet spoon, smooth the edges of each cookie into a rounded shape.

7. Bake 6 minutes. Reverse the pan so the back is in the front and bake 4 to 5 minutes more. The cookies appear lightly tan but not fully baked and with soft, pale centers. They will complete cooking on the warm baking sheet at room temperature. Shorter baking yields a chewier cookie while the longer time produces a crisper one. They will complete cooking as they cool.

8. Cool the cookies in the pan on a wire rack for 4 to 5 minutes. Remove the cookies with a spatula to a wire rack for complete cooling and firming.

9. In case a few remain, store in an airtight container or well-sealed plastic bag at cool room temperature.

YIELD: *a baker's dozen*

Peanut Butter and Oatmeal Jamwiches

This classic afterschool treat makes a grand lunch box snack, too. Our children preferred constructing their own creations with peanut butter and strawberry preserves.

½ cup all-purpose flour
¼ cup quick-cooking oatmeal
¼ teaspoon baking soda
⅓ cup packed light brown sugar
3 tablespoons granulated sugar
⅓ cup (5⅓ tablespoons) unsalted butter, softened
⅓ cup crunchy or smooth peanut butter
1 large egg yolk
½ teaspoon vanilla extract

1. With the rack in the center position, preheat the oven to 400°F.

2. Combine the flour with the oatmeal and baking soda and set aside.

3. In a small bowl, cream together both sugars with the butter, peanut butter, egg yolk, and vanilla until light and smooth.

4. With a wooden spoon or plastic scraper, combine the dry ingredients with the creamed mixture.

5. Drop by generous tablespoonfuls 2 inches apart onto a baking sheet. If desired, make crosshatch marks, gently pressing down with the tines of a fork dipped in sugar or flour.

6. Bake 4 minutes. Reverse the pan so the back is in the front and bake 4 minutes more. The cookies appear more baked around the edges than in the center. However, they will complete cooking on the warm sheet at room temperature.

7. Cool 2 minutes in the pan on a wire rack. With a spatula, remove the cookies to a wire rack for complete cooling. Fill and sandwich these just before serving so the cookies remain crisp.

8. Although the filling softens the cookie somewhat, wrap them well in plastic and store in the refrigerator or at cool room temperature. Unfilled cookies keep nicely in a plastic bag or an airtight container.

YIELD: *a baker's dozen*

FOR JAMWICHES

Spread a little peanut butter and preserves on the flat sides of 6 cookies. Top with the bottoms of the remaining cookies, gently pressing down to spread the filling. The extra cookie is the baker's reward!

❂ ❂ ❂
Miracles

When I set out to make these from a scrumptious-sounding idea, the first results worked perfectly—a miracle! Pulverized oatmeal, two different baking temperatures, and a trio of flavor-packed dried fruits produce these utterly delicious, crinkly topped treats. Although I prefer the dried fruit taste to shine, there's latitude for the addition of a favorite spice, such as nutmeg, cardamom, or mace.

½ cup plus 2 tablespoons and 2 teaspoons all-purpose flour
¼ cup quick-cooking or regular oats, pulverized to a flourlike consistency
¼ teaspoon baking soda
Pinch of salt
3 tablespoons unsalted butter, softened
¼ cup packed light brown sugar
2 tablespoons plus 2 teaspoons granulated sugar
1 large egg white
½ teaspoon vanilla extract
¼ cup tart dried cherries
3 tablespoons dried blueberries
2 tablespoons dried cranberries

1. With the rack positioned at the highest level, preheat the oven to 350°F. Lightly grease a cookie sheet with solid vegetable shortening.

2. Combine the flour, oats, baking soda, and salt. (This may be done in the food processor or blender when the oatmeal gets pulverized.) Set aside.

3. In a small bowl, cream the butter with both sugars, the egg white, and vanilla until light. (The mixture may appear curdled, but don't worry.)

4. Stir in the dry ingredients. Add the combined dried fruits and stir to distribute evenly throughout the batter.

5. Drop by generous tablespoonfuls in well-spaced mounds on a cookie sheet.

6. Bake 5 minutes. Reverse the cookie sheet so the back is in the front and increase the temperature to 400°F. Bake 3 to 4 minutes longer. The cookies are golden brown with a few pale spots.

7. Cool the cookies in the pan on a wire rack for 2 minutes. Remove the cookies with a spatula to a wire rack for complete cooling.

8. If any remain for storage, pack in a plastic bag or an airtight container.

Surprise Macaroons

This richly flavored peanut butter cookie sports crunchy edges and a soft center. Because the peanut butter flavor dominates, use margarine instead of butter, if you prefer. On humid days, it may be necessary to add more flour if the dough is loose. Add 1 teaspoonful at a time until the desired consistency is reached.

⅔ **cup plus 1 tablespoon all-purpose flour**
¼ **teaspoon baking soda**
Pinch of salt
3 tablespoons regular margarine or unsalted butter, softened
¼ **cup tightly packed light brown sugar**
4 tablespoons granulated sugar
⅓ **cup chunky or smooth peanut butter**
1 large egg white
1 teaspoon vanilla extract

1. With the rack in the highest position, preheat the oven to 375°F.

2. Combine the flour, baking soda, and salt and set aside.

3. In a small bowl, cream the margarine with the brown sugar, 3 tablespoons granulated sugar, peanut butter, egg white, and vanilla until light and fluffy.

4. With a fork or wooden spoon, stir in the dry ingredients until well blended.

5. Using a heaping tablespoonful of batter as a guide, make 12 large balls. Roll each ball in the remaining tablespoon of sugar. Place 2 inches apart on a cookie sheet. With a fork, make crosshatch marks on each cookie while flattening.

6. Bake 4 minutes. Reverse the cookie sheet so the back is in the front and continue baking 4 minutes longer.

7. Cool the cookies in the pan on a wire rack for 10 minutes. Remove the cookies to a wire rack for complete cooling.

8. For overnight storage, keep in an airtight container or well-sealed plastic bag at cool room temperature.

Potato Chip Cookies

This novelty cookie teases and surprises your taste buds with memories of shortbread. The combination of shortening and margarine produces the richest flavor and best texture.

¾ cup plus 1 tablespoon and 1 teaspoon all-purpose flour
¾ cup medium-fine hand-crushed potato chips
4 tablespoons (½ stick) regular corn oil margarine
3 tablespoons solid vegetable shortening
⅓ cup plus 1 teaspoon granulated sugar
1 teaspoon vanilla extract
⅓ cup chopped pecans or walnuts
1 tablespoon confectioners' sugar

1. With the rack in the center position, preheat the oven to 350°F.

2. Combine the flour with the crushed potato chips and set aside.

3. Cream the margarine and shortening with the granulated sugar and vanilla until smooth and light.

4. Using a fork or a wooden spoon, fold in the potato chip–flour mixture and nuts.

5. Using heaping teaspoonfuls as a guide and with dampened fingers, make 13 evenly sized balls. Place 2 inches apart on a cookie sheet. With dampened fingers or a water-dipped spoon, slightly flatten each one.

6. Bake 6 minutes. Reverse the pan so the back is in the front and bake 5 to 6 minutes more, or until the cookies are lightly golden with brown edges.

7. Cool in the pan on a wire rack for 2 minutes. Remove the cookies to a wire rack for complete cooling.

8. Dust with a sifting of confectioners' sugar before serving.

9. Store the cookies in an airtight container.

YIELD: *a baker's dozen*

Colonial Hermits

A gold mine of flavor awaits you in these lumpy, bumpy Early American cookies. Although I've never read why these were so named, I think it's because they're good keepers, a great packable treat for pioneers, prospectors, campers, and fishermen. Their great spicy flavor and moist, chewy texture get better during the long haul. This chunky interpretation contains dried apples—a fruit accessible to just about everyone in the colonies—and I think comes close to the heritage version that wives baked for their seafaring husbands during the early clipper ship days of our country. Molasses, naturally strong in flavor, dominates the aroma and taste in these cookies.

1 cup coarsely chopped, loosely packed dried apple chunks
¼ cup raisins or currants
¼ cup water, juice, or tea, for plumping
1 cup plus 1 tablespoon all-purpose flour
¼ teaspoon baking soda
¼ teaspoon cream of tartar
½ teaspoon ground cinnamon
Pinch of ground mace
Pinch of grated nutmeg
3 tablespoons regular corn oil margarine or solid vegetable shortening
¼ cup tightly packed dark brown sugar
2 tablespoons molasses
1 large egg yolk
3 tablespoons sour cream or buttermilk

Glaze

⅓ cup confectioners' sugar, sifted
2 to 3 teaspoons orange juice or cold coffee

1. With the rack in the center position, preheat the oven to 375°F. Grease a cookie sheet with solid vegetable shortening.

2. Combine the chopped apple chunks, raisins, and plumping liquid and set aside until all the liquid has been absorbed.

3. Combine the flour, baking soda, cream of tartar, cinnamon, mace, and nutmeg and set aside.

4. In a medium bowl, cream the margarine or shortening with the brown sugar and molasses. Beat in the egg yolk and sour cream or buttermilk until the mixture is smooth and liquid.

5. Stir in the dry ingredients. Fold in the plumped fruits.

6. Drop by heaping tablespoonfuls onto the prepared cookie sheet. Bake 7 minutes. Reverse the pan so the back is in the front and bake 5 to 6 minutes more. Test with a toothpick when the minimum baking time is up. If a few crumbs adhere to the tester, remove the cookies from the oven. The cookies continue baking as they cool.

7. Cool 2 minutes in the pan on a wire rack. Remove the cookies to a wire rack for complete cooling.

8. Prepare the glaze by stirring the confectioners' sugar with the orange juice or cold coffee until smooth. Brush on the cooled cookies.

9. These keep best when stored in the refrigerator in a plastic bag or tightly sealed container.

YIELD: *a baker's (or prospector's!) dozen*

✪ ✪ ✪
Glazed Banana Oatmeal Mounds

These wholesome, chewy little cakes travel well. Remember these for picnics, lunch boxes, and in the "I Love You" packages for your camper or exam-prepping student. A wonderful flavor develops during the few hours after they're baked. Although commercially dried orange peel is convenient to use here, it's easy to make your own zest from thick-skinned navel oranges, especially during the winter when they're plentiful.

¾ cup quick-cooking (not instant) oatmeal
¾ cup all-purpose flour
½ teaspoon grated nutmeg
¼ teaspoon baking soda
Pinch of salt
½ teaspoon orange zest or dried peel
⅓ cup coarsely chopped walnuts or pecans
4 tablespoons (½ stick) unsalted butter or regular corn oil margarine, softened
⅓ cup packed light brown sugar
1 large egg white
1 teaspoon vanilla extract
⅓ cup lightly packed mashed banana

Orange Juice Glaze

Scant ⅓ cup confectioners' sugar, sifted
2 to 3 teaspoons orange juice

1. With the rack in the highest position, preheat the oven to 375°F. Generously grease a cookie sheet with solid vegetable shortening.

2. Combine the oatmeal, flour, nutmeg, baking soda, salt, orange peel, and nuts and set aside.

3. Cream the butter or margarine with the sugar, egg white, and vanilla until light. Beat in the mashed banana until thoroughly mixed and fluffy.

4. Using a wooden spoon or fork, stir in the flour mixture until thoroughly combined.

5. Drop by heaping tablespoonfuls onto the prepared cookie sheet, leaving 2 inches between each one. With the back of a wet spoon, press the batter down lightly and smooth the edges of each cookie into a rounded shape.

6. Bake 7 minutes. Reverse the pan so the back is in the front and bake 5 minutes more. The cookies are a nice golden brown color and the surface appears dry. A toothpick inserted near the center will emerge clean.

7. Cool in the pan on a wire rack for 2 minutes.

8. Make the glaze by whisking the confectioners' sugar and orange juice together until smooth. Brush each warm cookie with the glaze.

9. Remove the cookies to a wire rack for complete cooling.

YIELD: *a baker's dozen*

✿ ✿ ✿
Almond Gazelles

I love this cookie because it is simply delicious. It could be my staff of life. Although I've searched almost the world over, I've never found a recipe and no professional baker has ever divulged any information, except to say "lots of almonds," for these chewy, solid almond, almond-encrusted, chocolate-tipped gazelles that give me great, sweet pleasure. The food processor makes them in moments and lining the baking sheet with aluminum foil helps the gazelles maintain their lovely, chubby curves.

1 8-ounce can almond paste
¾ cup granulated sugar
1 tablespoon plus 1 teaspoon all-purpose flour
¼ teaspoon baking powder
Pinch of salt
1 large egg white
1 teaspoon almond extract
¾ to 1 cup unblanched sliced almonds
⅓ cup semisweet chocolate chips
1 tablespoon unsalted butter

1. Position the rack in the upper third of the oven. Preheat the oven to 375°F. Line a cookie sheet with aluminum foil.

2. In the workbowl of the food processor, using the metal blade, process the almond paste, sugar, flour, baking powder, and salt until thoroughly combined and the mixture resembles sand.

3. With the machine running, pour the combined egg white and almond extract through the feed tube. The mixture will combine and clean the sides of the workbowl, about 20 to 30 seconds. Turn the mixture out onto a lightly floured work surface and knead until it comes together in a smooth mass. Roll into a 13-inch long rope. Using a ruler as a guide, cut the rope into 13 1-inch pieces. The mixture is sticky, so dip fingers in either water or flour.

4. Place the almonds on a large piece of wax paper.

5. For each gazelle, pinch off a piece of almond batter and form a ball. Gently roll the ball in the sliced almonds to coat completely. As you do this, the balls will form chubby 3- to 4-inch sausages. Place the almond-encrusted gazelles 2 inches apart on the cookie sheet. Gently press them down to flatten slightly. Curve the ends toward the center to form a crescent shape. If the cookies crack, pinch and push them back together.

6. Bake 7 minutes. Reverse the pan so the back is in the front and bake 6 minutes more, or until the cookies are lightly golden. The cooled texture is soft and chewy so do not overbake. Cookies continue baking as they cool.

7. Cool the cookies in the pan on a wire rack for about 5 to 8 minutes. Using a spatula, remove the cookies to a wire rack for complete cooling.

8. In a small saucepan over low heat, melt the chocolate chips and butter. Stir until smooth and shiny.

9. Using a small frosting knife, spread the chocolate lavishly on the ends of the gazelles. Place the cookies on wax paper or foil until the chocolate sets.

*YIELD: **a baker's dozen***

Salted Peanut Granola Cookies

These cookies are a little crunchy, a little chewy, with the surprise play of sweet and gently salty. Use your favorite granola in these delights.

¾ cup all-purpose flour
¼ teaspoon baking soda
1 teaspoon ground cinnamon
6 tablespoons (¾ stick) very soft unsalted butter
1 teaspoon honey or molasses
⅓ cup packed light brown sugar
1 large egg yolk
1 teaspoon vanilla extract
¾ cup granola
¼ cup coarsely chopped lightly salted peanuts

1. With the rack in the center position, preheat the oven to 350°F. Lightly gloss a cookie sheet with baking spray. Using a paper towel, remove the foam and spread the spray evenly over the pan.

2. Combine the flour, baking soda, and cinnamon and set aside.

3. Cream the butter with the honey or molasses, brown sugar, egg yolk, and vanilla until light.

4. Using a fork, thoroughly combine the creamed mixture with the reserved dry ingredients. Stir in the granola and peanuts, stirring to combine well. The dough is crumbly.

5. Using a heaping tablespoonful as a guide, shape the mixture with wet hands into 13 evenly sized balls or mounds. Place the mounds 2 inches apart on the prepared cookie sheet.

6. Bake 6 minutes. Reverse the pan and bake 6 to 7 minutes longer, or until the edges are dry. The centers will be soft and pale.

7. Cool in the pan on a wire rack for 4 to 5 minutes. Remove the cookies to a wire rack for complete cooling.

8. Store the cookies in an airtight container.

YIELD: a baker's dozen

Cowboy Cookies

*T*his substantial cookie, with both soft and crunchy areas, accommodates whatever combination of ingredients your family enjoys and you have on hand. It fesses up to other aliases, too, like "Kitchen Sink Cookies" and "Cookies of Last Resource."

¾ cup all-purpose flour
¼ teaspoon baking soda
Pinch of salt
5 tablespoons plus 2 teaspoons unsalted butter
⅓ cup packed light brown sugar
1 large egg white
1 teaspoon vanilla extract
½ cup crispy rice cereal
¼ cup quick-cooking oatmeal
¼ cup milk chocolate–covered raisins

1. With the rack in the center position, preheat the oven to 350°F.

2. Combine the flour, baking soda, and salt and set aside.

3. In a medium-sized bowl, using a handheld mixer, cream the butter with the sugar until light and smooth. Add the egg white and vanilla and continue beating until the mixture is creamy.

4. Using a fork or wooden spoon, stir in the flour mixture, cereal, oatmeal, and chocolate–covered raisins.

5. Using a heaping tablespoonful as a guide, shape the mixture with wet hands into 13 evenly sized balls or mounds. Place the mounds 2 inches apart on the prepared cookie sheet. Using a fork to make crosshatch marks, gently press down on each cookie to slightly flatten.

6. Bake 6 minutes. Reverse the pan so the back is in the front and bake 6 to 7 minutes longer, or until cookies spring back when lightly pressed.

7. Cool the cookies in the pan on a wire rack for 2 minutes. Remove the cookies to a wire rack for complete cooling.

YIELD: *a baker's dozen*

3

Southern Comforts

When I moved to the Shenandoah Valley of Virginia from New Jersey thirty-three years ago, my taste buds reawakened with the first taste of southern sweets. Covered-dish church socials and PTA potluck suppers were the specific destinations for my cookie discoveries.

I'd be willing to bet my weight in Old-Timey Traditional Preachers that no other region in our great country can claim concoctions as sublime and inventive as these. When unexpected guests came calling, ''a sweet something'' was immediately created from the odds and ends on hand. Steamy summer weather begot cookies that baked in the refrigerator and kept the kitchen cool.

Scarlett's Kisses
Old-Timey Traditional Preachers
Double Chocolate Peanut Preachers
Preachers Gone Astray
Preachers Gone Astray Truffles
Camel Bumps
Pecan Pie Bars
Chewy Coconut Bars
Delta Bars
Pecan Butter Cookies
Date Nut Chews
Pecan Lace
Golden Hermits
Toasted Marshmallow Mississippi Mud

Scarlett's Kisses

I enountered these for the first time several years ago at a Taste of Atlanta buffet dinner and I couldn't believe what I was experiencing. These delicate morsels bewitched me with their melting sweetness enveloping the crunch of toasted pecans. Because I was somewhere near Tara, I baptized them with that famous woman's name. If you're in New Orleans, ask for Praline Kisses and in Virginia, request Forgotten Kisses. Meringues do best in a totally grease-free, dry environment. A smidgen of fat causes collapse while humidity gets absorbed by the sugar, making the kisses sticky instead of chewy-crisp. Depending on how sweet you like these, you have latitude with the amount of light brown sugar to use.

1 large egg white, at room temperature
Pinch of salt
Pinch of cream of tartar
½ teaspoon vanilla extract
¼ to ⅓ cup packed light brown sugar
½ cup coarsely chopped pecans, toasted and cooled

1. With the rack positioned in the upper third of the oven, preheat the oven to 300°F. Prepare a cookie sheet by lining it with aluminum foil.

2. In a medium-sized bowl, with the mixer on medium speed, beat the egg white and salt until frothy. Add the cream of tartar and drizzle in the vanilla. Continue beating, increasing the speed to the highest level, until soft peaks form when the beaters are slowly lifted.

3. Gradually add the sugar by heaping tablespoonfuls and continue beating until the mixture is shiny and the peaks hold their points when the beaters are slowly lifted.

4. With a plastic scraper, gently fold in the nuts.

5. Using the tip of another teaspoon, push by heaping, rounded teaspoonfuls onto the prepared pan.

6. Bake 18 to 20 minutes. Turn off the oven and, without opening the oven door, leave the cookies in the oven for 5 to 7 minutes. Baked kisses are barely tan and firm to the touch.

7. Cool the cookies in the pan on a wire rack. When completely cool, transfer the cookies with a spatula to a wire rack. The cooled cookies will slide easily onto the spatula.

8. Store the kisses in an airtight container away from dampness.

Old-Timey Traditional Preachers

These unbaked cookies belong to a truly special, limited collection of regional recipes known as the South's sweetest secrets. Everyone loves them. Originally devised, it is said, decades ago by a gracious and clever Virginia housewife who needed a little treat for the preacher who came a-visiting unexpectedly. This peanut butter version is said to be the original and the one youngsters prefer. A school cafeteria cook I know says she produces thousands of these each year. Double up on the chopped pecans for those who prefer a cookie without coconut.

4 tablespoons (½ stick) unsalted butter
½ cup granulated sugar
2 tablespoons unsweetened baking cocoa
2 tablespoons milk
2 tablespoons crunchy or smooth peanut butter
½ cup quick-cooking oatmeal
2 tablespoons chopped pecans
2 tablespoons flaked or shredded coconut

1. Prepare the cookie sheet by lining with wax paper or aluminum foil.

2. In a small, heavy saucepan over moderate heat, stirring constantly, melt the butter with the sugar, cocoa, milk, and peanut butter. Bring to a full boil to dissolve the sugar. If the sugar doesn't dissolve, the cookies have a grainy texture and dull color. Cook at a full boil for 1½ minutes. Stir in the oatmeal and beat vigorously to combine. Remove the pan from the heat and quickly stir in the pecans and coconut.

3. Drop by heaping tablespoonfuls onto the prepared sheet.

4. Refrigerate or leave at cool room temperature until set.

5. Store in a plastic bag or airtight container at cool room temperature or in the refrigerator.

YIELD: *a baker's dozen*

Double Chocolate Peanut Preachers

These cookies represent my enlightened variation of the previous recipe. They quickly became my oldest son's favorite when he tasted them in kindergarten twenty-five years ago. Made in a pot on top of the stove, these fudgy winners contain neither flour nor eggs and "baking" takes place in the fridge.

4 tablespoons (½ stick) unsalted butter
½ cup granulated sugar
2 tablespoons milk
2 tablespoons unsweetened baking cocoa
¼ cup semisweet chocolate chips
½ cup quick-cooking oatmeal
¼ cup chopped salted peanuts

1. Prepare the cookie sheet by lining with wax paper or aluminum foil.

2. In a small, heavy saucepan over moderate heat, stirring constantly, melt the butter with the sugar, milk, cocoa, and chocolate chips. Bring to a full boil to dissolve the sugar. If the sugar doesn't dissolve, the cookies have a grainy texture and dull color. Cook at a full boil for 1½ minutes. Stir in the oatmeal and beat vigorously to combine. Remove the pan from the heat and quickly stir in the peanuts.

3. Drop by heaping tablespoonfuls onto the prepared sheet. Virginians prefer these lumpy. Should you prefer less mountainous cookies, flatten and round each mound with the back of the spoon.

4. Refrigerate or leave at cool room temperature until set.

5. Store in a plastic bag or airtight container at cool room temperature or in the refrigerator.

YIELD: *a baker's dozen*

Preachers Gone Astray

From a simple country cookie comes a rich morsel with tangy dried apricots woven throughout the chocolate. These remain softer than the other Preacher variations. You determine how sweet you like these.

4 tablespoons (½ stick) unsalted butter
⅓ to ½ cup granulated sugar
2 tablespoons milk
2 tablespoons unsweetened baking cocoa
½ cup quick-cooking oatmeal
2 tablespoons coarsely chopped toasted walnuts, pecans, or hazelnuts
⅓ cup chopped dried apricots (about 8 apricots)

1. Prepare the cookie sheet by lining with aluminum foil or wax paper.

2. In a small, heavy saucepan over moderate heat, stirring constantly, melt the butter with sugar, milk, and cocoa. Bring to full boil to dissolve the sugar. If the sugar doesn't dissolve, the cookies have a grainy texture and dull color. Cook at a full boil for 1½ minutes. Stir in the oatmeal and beat vigorously to combine. Remove the pan from the heat and quickly stir in the toasted nuts and apricots.

3. Drop by heaping tablespoonfuls onto the prepared pan.

4. Refrigerate or leave at cool room temperature until set.

YIELD: a baker's dozen

● ● ●

VARIATION ON A THEME

Preachers Gone Astray Truffles

1 to 2 teaspoonfuls of a liqueur
2 chocolate sandwich cookies, ground to a powder or ½ cup flaked or shredded
  coconut

1. Using the recipe for Preachers Gone Astray, macerate the chopped apricots in a favorite liqueur, such as Grand Marnier.

2. Continue with the recipe. Stir the soaked, drained fruits into the hot chocolate mixture. Drop by tablespoonfuls as above.

3. When cool enough to handle, roll each mound into a truffle ball. Roll each truffle in either the ground cookie crumbs or flaked coconut to coat completely.

4. Store in the refrigerator.

Camel Bumps

Young little hands have a grand time making these yummy cereal cookies, the name they are more often called. Our twin sons, Jeff and Hugo, gleefully named these when they were in kindergarten a long time ago. Use an assortment of cereals just for the fun of it.

2 tablespoons (¼ stick) regular corn oil margarine
¼ cup light corn syrup
2 tablespoons granulated sugar
½ cup semisweet chocolate chips
⅓ cup smooth or chunky peanut butter
½ teaspoon vanilla extract
2 cups your favorite flake cereal, such as cornflakes

1. In a heavy, flat-bottomed saucepan, melt the margarine with the corn syrup and sugar until the sugar liquefies.

2. Remove from the heat and quickly stir in the chocolate chips until they melt.

3. Stir in the peanut butter and vanilla and combine well.

4. With a wooden spoon, stir in the cereal, crushing and breaking the flakes while combining.

5. Drop by heaping tablespoonfuls onto a cookie sheet.

6. Leave at cool room temperature to set or refrigerate for 20 minutes, until the chocolate hardens and the bumps are no longer messy to eat.

7. Store at cool room temperature or in the refrigerator.

YIELD: *a baker's dozen*

Pecan Pie Bars

A favorite pie's ingredients are sandwiched between wonderful layers of brown sugar shortbread.

Shortbread

1¼ cups plus 3 tablespoons all-purpose flour
Pinch of salt
8 tablespoons (1 stick) unsalted butter, softened
½ cup packed light brown sugar
1 teaspoon vanilla extract

Filling

2 tablespoons (¼ stick) unsalted butter, melted
1 large egg
⅓ cup dark corn syrup
¼ cup granulated sugar
1 teaspoon vanilla extract
1 cup coarsely chopped pecans

1. With the rack in the center position, preheat the oven to 350°F. Gloss an 8 × 8-inch pan with baking spray. Using a paper towel, remove the foam and spread the spray evenly over the pan.

2. Prepare the shortbread. Combine 1¼ cups flour and salt and set aside. In a small bowl, cream the butter with the brown sugar and vanilla until light and creamy.

3. Using a table fork, stir in the dry ingredients until the mixture becomes crumbly.

4. Reserve ½ cup of packed dough. Press the remaining dough into the prepared pan. The dough should be even and level without a rim or stand-up edge. Bake 18 minutes.

5. While the base is baking, add the remaining 3 tablespoons of flour to the reserved dough. Using a fork, cut the flour into the dough to form crumbs. Set aside. (If the mixture has become too soft, place in the freezer.)

6. Prepare the filling. In a small bowl, combine the melted butter with the egg, dark corn syrup, and sugar. Stir in the vanilla and pecans.

7. Remove the crust from the oven. Reduce the oven temperature to 300°F. Pour or spoon the pecan filling over the hot dough from edge to edge. Sprinkle the crumbs evenly and completely over the pecan filling. Gently press down on the crumbs.

8. Bake 45 to 50 minutes, or until lightly golden brown.

9. Cool the pan on a wire rack for 20 minutes. Cut into bars. Cool the bars completely before removing from the pan.

10. Store the bars in an airtight container.

YIELD: 12 large or 16 medium bars

VARIATION ON A THEME

Chewy Coconut Bars

Use the following filling in place of the pecan pie filling.

1 large egg
⅓ cup packed light brown sugar
1 tablespoon all-purpose flour
½ teaspoon vanilla extract
⅔ cup flaked coconut

1. Combine the egg with the brown sugar, flour, and vanilla. Stir in the coconut.

2. Pour over the hot crust. Continue with the directions as outlined above.

3. Bake 45 to 50 minutes.

Delta Bars

This is the real song of the South—shortbread, pecans, and brown sugar meringue all in one. Had Scarlett made a plate of these for Rhett, he'd never have left.

¾ cup all-purpose flour
½ teaspoon baking powder
¼ teaspoon salt

6 tablespoons (¾ stick) unsalted butter
⅓ cup plus ¼ cup packed light brown sugar
1 large egg yolk
1 cup coarsely chopped pecans

Topping

1 large egg white
Pinch of salt
½ teaspoon vanilla extract

1. With the rack in the center position, preheat the oven to 350°F. Gloss an 8 × 8-inch pan with baking spray. Using a paper towel, remove the foam and spread the spray evenly over the pan.

2. Combine the flour, baking powder, and salt and set aside.

3. Cream the butter and ⅓ cup brown sugar. Add the egg yolk. Gradually work the flour mixture in until the ingredients are crumbly. Stir in ½ cup of the chopped pecans. Press the mixture into the prepared pan. Bake 10 minutes.

4. Meanwhile, in a clean bowl with clean beaters, beat the egg white until frothy. Add a pinch of salt. Continue beating until very soft peaks form.

5. Beat in the vanilla and gradually add ¼ cup brown sugar. If the sugar is added too quickly, the peaks will flop. Do not despair. Use them anyway; the bars will taste just as good even if the topping is not lofty. Continue beating only until the egg white is smooth and shiny with soft peaks. Fold in the remaining pecans.

6. Smooth the mixture over the hot shortbread to cover completely.

7. Bake 20 to 25 minutes, or just until the surface is firm.

8. Remove from the oven and cut into bars while still hot.

9. Store in a tightly covered container or securely wrapped in plastic.

YIELD: *12 large or 16 medium bars*

Pecan Butter Cookies

This is the quintessential nut cookie—crisp, buttery, and nutty.

⅔ **cup plus 1 tablespoon all-purpose flour**
¼ **teaspoon baking powder**
5 **tablespoons unsalted butter, softened**
⅓ **cup granulated sugar**
1 **teaspoon vanilla extract**
½ **cup finely chopped pecans**

1. With the rack in the center position, preheat the oven to 375°F.

2. Combine the flour with the baking powder and set aside.

3. Cream the butter with the sugar and vanilla until creamy and light.

4. Using your fingers or a fork, work the dry ingredients into the creamed mixture until the dough cleans the bowl and forms a ball.

5. Hand knead in the nuts.

6. Use generously rounded teaspoonfuls as a guide to make 13 uniformly sized balls. Place them 2 inches apart on a cookie sheet. Flatten the cookies with a lightly greased glass base dipped in granulated sugar or with a deeply indented ceramic cookie stamp.

7. Bake 6 minutes. Reverse the pan so the back is in the front and bake 4 to 5 minutes longer, or until the cookies are light golden.

8. Cool the cookies in the pan on a wire rack for 2 minutes. Remove the cookies to a wire rack for complete cooling.

9. Store these delights in an airtight container.

YIELD: *a baker's dozen*

✪ ✪ ✪
Date Nut Chews

Although I've outlined the standard method for mixing these snowy balls of chewy sweetness, I prefer to make mine the fast and easy way in the food processor. First chop the dates and nuts with a little of the flour. Then add all of the remaining ingredients and process until everything is reduced to tiny particles. Remember to use the ⅓ cup measure twice when measuring ⅔ cup.

4 tablespoons (½ stick) unsalted butter
2 tablespoons granulated sugar
½ teaspoon vanilla extract
⅔ cup all-purpose flour
⅔ cup pecan halves, finely chopped
½ cup whole dates, finely chopped (about 12 whole dates)
½ cup confectioners' sugar, sifted

1. With the rack in the center position, preheat the oven to 350°F.

2. Cream the butter and sugar until well combined and light. Beat in the vanilla.

3. Stir in the flour. Add the chopped pecans and chopped dates. Using your hands or a wooden spoon, combine the mixtures well. The dough is crumbly but it will mold together.

4. Using wet fingers, make 13 evenly sized balls and place on a cookie sheet. These don't grow during baking, thus only a bit of space between each one is required.

5. Bake 5 minutes. Reverse the pan so the back is in the front and bake 4 to 5 minutes longer.

6. Cool the cookies in the pan on a wire rack for 10 minutes. Place the confectioners' sugar in a bag. Carefully place a few cookies at a time in the bag and gently shake to evenly coat the balls with sugar. Remove the balls to a wire rack for complete cooling. They may need another coating of confectioners' sugar before serving.

7. Store these sweet morsels in an airtight container.

YIELD: *a baker's dozen*

Pecan Lace

*T*hese crispy cookies are a sweet dream-come-true for pecan lovers. Completely cool these delicate delights on the cookie sheet before removing. Otherwise you will become exasperated because too many cookies will shatter into crumbs.

1 cup medium-fine chopped pecans
2 tablespoons plus 1 teaspoon all-purpose flour
2 tablespoons (¼ stick) unsalted butter
3 tablespoons dark or light corn syrup
1 tablespoon tightly packed light brown sugar

1. With the rack in the center position, preheat the oven to 350°F. Prepare the cookie sheet by lining it with aluminum foil.

2. Combine the chopped pecans with the flour and set aside.

3. In a small heavy saucepan over medium heat, melt the butter with the corn syrup and brown sugar. While stirring, bring to a rolling boil. (The mixture will appear as if it has thickened and lightened.)

4. Remove the pan from the heat. Stir the pecans and flour into the hot sugar mixture. Stir to combine thoroughly.

5. Drop by rounded teaspoonfuls 2 to 3 inches apart onto the prepared pan.

6. Bake 5 minutes. Reduce the oven temperature to 325°F. Reverse the pan so the back is in the front and bake 5 to 6 minutes longer. The cookies will be golden with darker edges. (The cookies will darken more as they cool.) If the cookies have met each other all over the pan, use a large biscuit cutter to quickly and gently push them into separate round shapes as soon as you take them out of the oven.

7. Cool the cookies completely in the pan on a wire rack. They will slide onto a spatula easily when cooled.

8. Store in a plastic bag or container with a loose-fitting lid between sheets of wax paper.

YIELD: *a baker's dozen*

Golden Hermits

The suggestion for this recipe, an early American dried fruit cookie made into chewy bars, came from a friend whose Scotch-Irish ancestors were among the first to settle in the Shenandoah Valley of Virginia. She remembers her grandmother and father preparing something like this and calling them "hermits" because they stayed moist for as long as they lasted. This made them perfect for taking on trips or for packing in the lunch pail as the field hands' afternoon snack—or, as the name implies, for taking to the mountains when you wanted to get away from it all. Golden Hermits combine the tasty elements the Scots are devoted to: oatmeal, buttery shortbread, and brown sugar. Dried apricots chop easily in the food processor using the metal blade with the pulse technique. Alternatively, gloss the blade of a heavy knife with nonstick cooking spray and chop away.

Shortbread

⅓ cup all-purpose flour
1½ cups quick-cooking oatmeal
⅓ cup packed light brown sugar
7 tablespoons unsalted butter, softened

Topping

2 large eggs
2 tablespoons orange or lemon juice
½ teaspoon vanilla extract
⅓ cup packed light brown sugar
3 tablespoons all-purpose flour
½ teaspoon baking powder
1 cup tightly packed whole dried apricots, finely chopped
2 tablespoons confectioners' sugar, sifted

1. With the rack in the center position, preheat the oven to 350°F. Lightly butter an 8 × 8-inch pan.

2. In a small bowl, combine the flour, oatmeal, and sugar. Cut in the butter until the mixture is mealy. Reserve ⅓ cup and press the remainder firmly into the prepared pan. Bake 18 to 20 minutes, or until lightly golden.

3. Meanwhile, using the same bowl, beat the eggs with the juice, vanilla, brown sugar, flour, and baking powder. Stir in the apricots. Pour the mixture over the hot crust, spreading it evenly from edge to edge. Strew the reserved oatmeal crumbs over the filling. Bake about 35 minutes, or until the top is golden and the edges are burnished.

4. Cool completely on a wire rack. Shower with a sifting of confectioners' sugar before cutting into bars.

5. These are sure to disappear quickly. For the few you may want to hide, store well wrapped or in an airtight container.

*YIELD: **12 large or 16 medium bars***

⚡ ⚡ ⚡

Toasted Marshmallow Mississippi Mud

These are always a big hit at bake sales, pj parties, and whenever you need a killer sweet. Overnight aging develops the flavor and makes the Mud easier to cut. Toasted marshmallows add flavor dimension—as if it needs more!

Brownie

¾ cup all-purpose flour
¼ teaspoon salt
8 tablespoons (1 stick) unsalted butter
¼ cup unsweetened baking cocoa
¾ cup granulated sugar
1 teaspoon vanilla extract
2 large eggs, slightly beaten
¾ cup coarsely chopped pecans
1 cup miniature marshmallows

Frosting

3 tablespoons unsalted butter
3 tablespoons unsweetened baking cocoa
2 to 3 tablespoons heavy cream or evaporated milk
1 teaspoon vanilla extract
1 to 1⅓ cups sifted confectioners' sugar

1. With the rack in the center position, preheat the oven to 350°F. Gloss an 8 × 8-inch pan with baking spray. Using a paper towel, remove the foam and spread the spray evenly over the pan.

2. Combine the flour with the salt and set aside.

3. In a small saucepan over low heat, melt the butter. Add the cocoa and stir until smooth. Remove the the pan from the heat and stir in the sugar, vanilla, and eggs until the mixture is well combined. Add the flour and salt and stir until thoroughly mixed. The mixture will be thick and gooey.

4. Scrape the batter into the prepared pan. Strew the chopped pecans over the top and from edge to edge. Bake 23 to 25 minutes, or until a tester comes out clean.

5. Increase the oven temperature to 400°F. Strew the miniature marshmallows on top of the hot cake from edge to edge. Return the cake to the oven for 3 minutes, or until the marshmallows are golden. Remove the cake from the oven and place on a wire rack.

6. Meanwhile, prepare the frosting. In a small saucepan over low heat, melt the butter. Whisk in the cocoa and the minimum quantity of cream or milk, stirring until smooth. Remove the pan from the heat and whisk in 1 cup of the confectioners' sugar and vanilla, stirring until smooth and shiny, adding more sugar if necessary. Pour slowly over the hot cake from edge to edge and covering the marshmallows.

7. Cool the Mud completely in the pan on a wire rack. When completely cooled, cover with aluminum foil and let it "age" overnight. Cut into bars the next day.

8. If there are any remnants, store at cool room temperature covered with aluminum foil.

YIELD: 12 large or 16 medium bars

DOLORES KOSTELNI

4

Sweet Nothings

*T*hese small succulent clouds are made from the marriage of egg whites and sugar whipped to lofty heights. An absence of fat makes them the calorie counter's favorite sweet. Make no mistake, though, their chewy crispness beguiles and tantalizes. Versatile and amenable, they drop from a spoon, they roll and cut, and they pipe from a pastry bag to form stars, hearts, and wreaths.

Peanut Butter Coconut Kisses
Pecan Date Kisses
Siren's Kisses
Coconut Angels
Lemon Buttons
Chocolate Buttons

Peanut Butter Coconut Kisses

Surprisingly light, these puff nicely during baking. The finished cookie has a creamy center surrounded by a lightly crisp exterior.

1 large egg white, at room temperature
Pinch of salt
Pinch of cream of tartar
⅓ cup granulated sugar
⅓ cup smooth or chunky peanut butter, melted and cooled
⅔ cup flaked or grated coconut

1. With the rack in the center position, preheat the oven to 300°F. Prepare a cookie sheet by lining it with aluminum foil.

2. In a medium bowl with the mixer on medium speed, beat the egg white with the salt until foamy. Add the cream of tartar and beat at high speed until sturdy soft peaks form when the beaters are slowly lifted.

3. Gradually stream in the sugar by heaping tablespoonfuls and continue beating until the mixture is shiny and peaks hold their points when the beaters are slowly lifted.

4. Fold in the peanut butter and coconut.

5. Using the tip of another teaspoon, push the mixture by heaping teaspoonfuls onto the prepared pan.

6. Bake 20 to 25 minutes. The finished kisses are golden and firm to the touch.

7. Cool in the pan on a wire rack. When completely cool, transfer the cookies with a spatula to a wire rack.

8. Store the finished kisses in an airtight container or plastic bag away from dampness.

Pecan Date Kisses

Light, chewy, and sweet, like the little nothings they feasted on in the Arabian Nights. *For best results, make these on dry, moistureproof days. An easy way to chop the dates and nuts is to place them in the food processor and pulse ON/OFF until a fine consistency is reached. Large pieces of dates often get jawbreaker hard in meringues.*

1 large egg white, at room temperature
Scant pinch of salt
Pinch of cream of tartar
¼ teaspoon vanilla extract
Few drops of orange extract
¼ cup packed light brown sugar
1 tablespoon granulated sugar
½ cup finely chopped pitted dates
½ cup finely chopped pecans

1. With the rack in the center position, preheat the oven to 300°F. Prepare the cookie sheet by lining it with aluminum foil.

2. In a completely grease-free medium-sized bowl with the mixer on medium speed, beat the egg white and salt until frothy. Add the cream of tartar and drizzle in the combined vanilla and orange extracts. Continue beating, increasing the speed to highest level, until soft peaks form (the points will tip over) when the beaters are slowly lifted.

3. Gradually add the brown and granulated sugars by heaping tablespoonfuls and continue beating until the mixture is shiny and peaks hold their points when the beaters are slowly lifted.

4. With a plastic scraper, gently fold in the combined dates and pecans.

5. Using the back of another teaspoon, push by heaping rounded teaspoonfuls onto the prepared pan.

6. Bake 20 minutes. Without opening the door, turn off the oven and leave the cookies in the oven for an additional 10 minutes. The finished kisses are pale golden brown and firm on top when lightly pressed.

7. Cool the cookies in the pan on a wire rack. Transfer the cookies with a spatula to a wire rack.

8. Store the finished cookies in an airtight container away from dampness.

YIELD: a baker's dozen

Siren's Kisses

Serve these chocolate meringues as part of a buffet dessert with assorted fresh fruits, grated coconut, and warm chocolate sauce. Refine regular granulated sugar with confectioners' sugar by whirling together in the food processor or blender. Superfine sugar makes the lightest meringues. Because European-style cocoa is treated with an alkali, it remains true to its original dark color even after having been combined with the pure white meringue and baked. It gives these bewitching, alluring, lightly crisp, and gooey-centered beauties a richer final color and flavor.

Kisses

1 large egg white, at room temperature
Pinch of salt
Pinch of cream of tartar
½ teaspoon vanilla extract
⅓ cup superfine granulated sugar, free of lumps
2 tablespoons confectioners' sugar, sifted
1 tablespoon plus 1 teaspoon European-style baking cocoa
⅓ cup miniature semisweet chocolate chips

Topping

¹⁄₃ cup semisweet chocolate chips, melted and cooled
2 to 3 tablespoons unsalted butter, melted and cooled
2 tablespoons finely chopped pecans or walnuts

1. With the rack positioned in the upper third of the oven, preheat the oven to 300°F. Prepare a cookie sheet by lining it with aluminum foil.

2. In a medium-sized bowl with the mixer on medium speed, beat the egg white and salt until frothy. Add the cream of tartar and drizzle in the vanilla. Continue beating, increasing the speed to the highest level, until soft peaks form when the beaters are slowly lifted.

3. Gradually add the combined sugars by heaping tablespoonfuls. Continue beating until the mixture is shiny and peaks hold their points when the beaters are slowly lifted.

4. Using a small, grease-free tea strainer, sift the cocoa over the meringue. With a plastic scraper, gently fold in the cocoa. Fold in the miniature chocolate chips.

5. Using the tip of another teaspoon, push by rounded heaping teaspoonfuls onto the prepared pan.

6. Bake 18 to 20 minutes. A chocolate fragrance will waft through your kitchen. The baked kisses are brown and firm to the touch.

7. Cool the cookies in the pan on a wire rack. When completely cool, frost the cookies on the cookie sheet. Transfer the frosted cookies to a wire rack.

8. In a small saucepan over the lowest heat, melt the chocolate chips with the butter. Stir until smooth and glossy. Using a small spoon or knife, frost the top of each kiss. Sprinkle each kiss with finely chopped nuts.

9. When the chocolate has set, store the finished kisses in an airtight container away from dampness.

⚡ ⚡ ⚡
Coconut Angels

These light, airy meringues are dense with coconut. They produce an exquisite taste sensation, combining a gentle crunch with a seductively gooey center.

1 large egg white, at room temperature
Pinch of salt
½ teaspoon vanilla extract
Pinch of cream of tartar
⅓ cup granulated sugar
⅔ cup shredded or flaked coconut

1. With the rack positioned in the upper third of the oven, preheat the oven to 300°F. Prepare a cookie sheet by lining it with aluminum foil.

2. In a medium-sized bowl with the mixer on medium speed, beat the egg white with the salt and vanilla until foamy. Add the cream of tartar and beat at high speed until sturdy, soft peaks form when the beaters are slowly lifted.

3. Gradually add the sugar by heaping tablespoonfuls and continue beating until the mixture is shiny and peaks hold their points when the beaters are slowly lifted.

4. Using a plastic scraper, gently fold in the coconut.

5. Using the tip of another spoon, push by rounded tablespoonfuls onto the prepared pan.

6. Bake 20 minutes. The finished cookies are gently tanned and firm to the touch.

7. Cool in the pan on a wire rack. When completely cool, transfer the cookies with a spatula to a wire rack.

8. Store the cookies in an airtight container away from dampness.

YIELD: *a baker's dozen*

Lemon Buttons

Use a pastry bag outfitted with a star tip and pipe these basic meringue cookies with glistening jewel-like centers into beautiful love knots or stars. Jars of lemon curd, imported from England, are found in the gourmet food sections of most supermarkets. I recommend using imitation vanilla flavoring in this recipe because it does not tint the snowy white meringue with any degree of straw color. The finished cookie has a delicately crisp exterior with a soft, succulent center.

1 large egg white, at room temperature
Pinch of salt
½ teaspoon imitation clear vanilla extract
Pinch of cream of tartar
⅓ cup granulated sugar
Lemon curd

1. With the rack in the center position, preheat the oven to 200°F. Prepare a cookie sheet by lining it with aluminum foil.

2. In a medium-sized bowl with the mixer on medium speed, beat the egg white with the salt and vanilla until foamy. Add the cream of tartar and beat at high speed until sturdy soft peaks form when the beaters are slowly lifted.

3. Gradually add the sugar by heaping tablespoonfuls and continue beating until the mixture is shiny and peaks hold their points when the beaters are slowly lifted.

4. Using the tip of another teaspoon, push by rounded teaspoonfuls onto the prepared pan.

5. Using the rounded side of a ¼ teaspoon measuring spoon or demitasse spoon, make small round craters in the center of each cookie.

6. Bake 30 to 35 minutes. The finished cookies should be white and firm to the touch. Depending on your oven, it may be necessary to lower the temperature and increase the baking time by 10 to 15 minutes in order to get firm cookies.

7. Cool in the pan on a wire rack. When completely cool, fill each cookie with ¼ to ½ teaspoon of commercially prepared lemon curd.

8. These are best served within a few hours of completing. The filling softens the meringue, so they do not store well.

YIELD: a baker's dozen

VARIATION ON A THEME

Chocolate Buttons

1. Prepare the meringue cookies as directed above.

2. When completely cool, fill the craters with the following:

3 tablespoons semisweet chocolate chips
2 teaspoons butter

3. In a small saucepan over low heat, melt the chocolate chips and butter, stirring constantly until smooth and glossy. Cool slightly.

4. Fill each crater with the melted chocolate. Set aside for the chocolate to firm.

5. Serve within a few hours of filling.

5

Chocolate, Chocolate, and More Chocolate

All the world loves chocolate and these intensely flavored creations nurture that passion. Soft and fudgy riches like Chocolate Doubleheaders and Chocolate Chip Chocolate Drops are casual enough to make for PTA bake sales and sufficiently elegant for taking their deserved places on a special dessert tray.

Although more of a confection than a cookie, but too luscious to omit on a technicality, Chocolate Peanut Butter Pizza, made without baking, will become an indispensable family favorite—children's play, indeed!

Imagine luscious almonds and chocolate in a perfect union as Chocolate Macaroons or The Most Chocolate Brownies mated with an abundance of soft, melting semisweet chips and a lacing of raspberry preserves, or perhaps with a hidden lagoon of pecan pie filling. Elegant and extravagantly flavored, these fantastic cookies combine the best of all worlds.

Chocolate Doubleheaders

Rich, soft, and chewy, these are the best thing that's happened to chocolate in a long time. The unusual timing technique in mixing the separated egg into the batter is the reason these are so wonderful.

½ cup semisweet chocolate chips
1 ounce (1 square) unsweetened chocolate
2 tablespoons unsalted butter
3 tablespoons all-purpose flour
⅛ teaspoon (a healthy pinch) baking powder
Pinch of salt
⅓ cup plus 2 tablespoons granulated sugar
1 large egg, separated
1 teaspoon vanilla extract
¼ cup medium-fine chopped pecans, hazelnuts, or walnuts

DOLORES KOSTELNI

1. With the rack in the center position, preheat oven to 350°F. Lightly grease a cookie sheet with solid vegetable shortening.

2. In a small saucepan over low heat or in a microwave oven following manufacturer's directions, melt the chocolate chips, unsweetened chocolate, and butter together. Stir until smooth. Remove from the heat and set aside to cool.

3. Combine the flour, baking powder, and salt and set aside.

4. Beat the sugar with the egg white until smooth and creamy.

5. Continue beating while spooning in the still warm butter and chocolate.

6. Beat in the egg yolk and vanilla. Mix until smooth.

7. Stir in the dry ingredients. Add the nuts and combine well.

8. Drop by rounded tablespoonfuls 2 inches apart on the baking sheet. Using the back of a spoon or knife, smooth and round the mounds.

9. Bake 5 minutes. Reverse the pan so the back is in the front and bake 4 minutes longer. The cookies will give every indication of not being done. However, they will finish baking on the warm pan at room temperature.

10. Cool completely in the pan on a wire rack.

11. Store any leftovers in an airtight container at cool room temperature or in the refrigerator.

YIELD: *a baker's dozen*

Chocolate Macaroons

Here is one of the world's most elegant cookies in a simplified interpretation. Because of the chocolate, this mixture is sticky and thick, but like the Positano Amaretti and the Italian Pastry Shop Almond Macaroons, these can be plopped from a spoon or piped through a pastry bag with either a plain or large star tip. The finished cookie is light and crackly-topped with a soft, dark, chewy interior. It's absolutely necessary that the slivered almonds get pulverized to a powder before mixing with the egg white and chocolate.

⅔ cup blanched slivered almonds
½ cup granulated sugar
2 tablespoons confectioners' sugar, sifted
Pinch of salt
½ teaspoon almond extract
¼ teaspoon vanilla extract
1 large egg white
½ ounce (½ square) unsweetened chocolate, melted and cooled

1. With the rack in the center position, preheat the oven to 375°F. Line a cookie sheet with aluminum foil. Coat the foil with baking spray. Using a paper towel, rub the foam over the foil until it is evenly distributed and the surface is glossy.

2. Using a food processor outfitted with the metal blade, process the almonds with the sugars and salt until the mixture is powdery.

3. Add the almond and vanilla extracts to the egg white. With the food processor running, pour the egg white mixture through the feed tube. Using a plastic scraper, scrape the mixture up from the bottom and around the sides of the workbowl. Remove the food processor cover and scrape the cooled chocolate over the almond and egg white mixture. Process with several ON/OFF pulses until the batter is uniformly dark.

4. Using a teaspoon dipped in water for each cookie, push the batter off the spoon with the tip of another teaspoon in rounded mounds onto the prepared pan. Smooth any points and rough spots.

5. Bake 5 minutes. Reverse the pan so the back is in the front and bake 5 minutes longer. The cookies are done when they are puffy with a crackled surface.

6. Cool the cookies completely in the pan on a wire rack. When completely cool, remove by sliding the wide edge of a spatula under each cookie.

7. Store the cookies in an airtight container.

YIELD: a baker's dozen

Chocolate Marbles

*T*hese perfect little rounds are streaked with dark chocolate and contrasting vanilla highlights. Orange extract and a bit of sprightly zest gently underscore their flavor. For gussied-up marbles, sandwich with a filling of melted chocolate.

⅔ **cup plus 1 tablespoon all-purpose flour**
¼ **teaspoon baking powder**
Pinch of salt
4 tablespoons (½ stick) butter
⅓ **cup granulated sugar**
1 large egg yolk
2 teaspoons milk
¼ **teaspoon vanilla extract**
¼ **teaspoon orange extract**
¼ **cup semisweet chocolate chips, melted and cooled**
½ **teaspoon grated orange zest**

1. With the rack in the highest position, preheat the oven to 400°F.

2. Combine the flour, baking powder, and salt and set aside.

3. Cream the butter until light. Stream in the sugar and beat until fluffy. Add the egg yolk, milk, and vanilla and orange extracts.

4. With a wooden spoon or fork, stir in the dry ingredients until thoroughly combined and the mixture cleans the bowl. Slightly flatten the batter.

5. Combine the melted chocolate chips with the orange zest. Pour the cooled mixture onto the cookie batter in the bowl. With a fork, streak one batter into the other to get a marbled effect, with the chocolate dominating.

6. Drop the dough by heaping tablespoonfuls onto the cookie sheet. Using the back of a wet spoon, smooth each into a round shape.

7. Reduce the oven temperature to 350°F. Bake the cookies 5 minutes. Reverse the pan so the back is in the front and bake 4 to 5 minutes more. The cookies will have light golden edges and a crackled surface.

8. Cool the cookies in the pan on a wire rack for 4 minutes. Remove the cookies to a wire rack for complete cooling.

9. If any cookies remain, keep in a tightly sealed container.

YIELD: **a baker's dozen**

The Most Chocolate Brownies

Make this quickly, stirring only, not beating, in one bowl or a small saucepan. A fair warning to all who dare indulge in these dark beauties: Servings are the size of acres and I'll bet you can't stop with one!

3 ounces (3 squares) unsweetened chocolate
6 tablespoons (¾ stick) unsalted butter
⅔ cup all-purpose flour
Pinch of salt
1⅓ cups granulated sugar
3 large eggs, beaten
1 teaspoon vanilla extract
¾ cup semisweet chocolate chips

1. With the rack in the center position, preheat the oven to 325°F. Gloss an 8 × 8-inch pan with baking spray. Using a paper towel, rub the foam over the pan until it is evenly distributed and the surface is glossy.

2. In a small, heavy saucepan over low heat, melt the unsweetened chocolate and butter. Stir to combine smoothly. Remove from the heat and allow to cool slightly.

3. Combine the flour and salt and set aside.

4. In the saucepan containing the chocolate, gradually stir in the sugar off the heat. Add the eggs and vanilla. Stir only enough to combine. Fold in the flour mixture. The batter will be thick and gooey.

5. Smooth into the prepared pan. Strew the chocolate chips evenly over the surface.

6. Bake 33 to 34 minutes, or until a toothpick inserted at the center emerges with fudgy crumbs clinging to it. Remove the brownies from the oven immediately. The brownies will continue cooking for several minutes at room temperature. With a frosting knife, smooth and swirl the softened chocolate chips over the surface to form a glaze. Alternatively, leave the chips to cool without spreading them.

7. Store the brownies tightly covered.

YIELD: *12 large or 16 medium squares*

VARIATIONS ON A THEME

Luscious Raspberry Brownies

Filling

⅓ cup raspberry preserves, warm and liquid

1. Prepare The Most Chocolate Brownies through step 4.

2. Using a scraper, spread half of the batter into the prepared pan.

3. Pour the warmed preserves evenly over the batter, using a scraper, if necessary, to spread it.

4. Spread the remaining brownie batter evenly over the preserves, spreading it from corner to corner with a scraper. (Thin ribbons of the preserves may show through, but don't worry.)

5. Strew the chocolate chips evenly over the surface.

6. Bake 33 to 34 minutes. Test for doneness by inserting a tester or toothpick in the center. If several crumbs adhere to the tester, remove the brownies from the oven immediately. The brownies will continue cooking for several minutes at room temperature. With a frosting knife, spread and swirl the softened chocolate chips over the surface to form a glaze. Alternatively, leave the chips to cool without spreading them.

7. Store the brownies tightly covered.

Cream Cheese and Jelly–Stuffed Brownies

Filling

3 ounces cream cheese, softened
3 tablespoons granulated sugar
½ teaspoon vanilla extract
⅓ cup raspberry or strawberry preserves, warmed

1. Prepare the filling by beating the cream cheese with the sugar and vanilla until well combined. Set aside.

2. Prepare The Most Chocolate Brownies through step 4.

3. Smooth half of the batter into the prepared pan.

4. Using a scraper, distribute the cream cheese filling evenly over the brownie batter, leaving about a 1¼-inch border around the edges. Pour the warmed preserves evenly over the cream cheese, using a scraper, if necessary, to spread it.

5. Spread the remaining brownie batter evenly over the preserves, spreading it from corner to corner with a scraper. Strew the chocolate chips evenly over the surface.

6. Bake 25 to 30 minutes, or until a toothpick inserted at the center emerges with a few crumbs.

7. Swirl the melted chocolate chips over the brownie surface as instructed. Cool before cutting into bars.

Chocolate Mint Brownies

Mint Layer

2 tablespoons (¼ stick) unsalted butter, softened
¾ cup sifted confectioners' sugar
1 tablespoon crème de menthe
¼ teaspoon vanilla extract

Curlicue Glaze

¾ cup semisweet chocolate chips
2 tablespoons unsalted butter

1. Prepare The Most Chocolate Brownies, omitting the chocolate chips. Bake as instructed, testing at the minimum baking time. Cool the brownies in the pan on a wire rack.

2. Prepare the Mint Layer by creaming the softened butter with the confectioners' sugar until light. Beat in the crème de menthe and vanilla. Spread evenly over the cooled brownies. Refrigerate about 1 hour for the topping to set.

3. Prepare the Curlicue Glaze by melting the chocolate chips with butter in a small saucepan over low heat until the chocolate melts. Remove from the heat and stir until smooth and glossy. Drizzle in curlicues over the Mint Layer.

4. Refrigerate at least 1 hour before cutting into squares.

Pecan Pie–Stuffed Brownies

Filling

1 5-ounce jar pecans-in-syrup ice cream topping

1. Prepare The Most Chocolate Brownies through step 4.

2. Using a scraper, spread half of the batter into the prepared pan.

3. Pour the jar of pecans-in-syrup over the batter, using a scraper, if necessary, to spread it evenly.

4. Spread the remaining brownie batter evenly over the filling, spreading it from corner to corner with a scraper. (Thin ribbons of filling may show through, but don't worry.)

5. Strew the chocolate chips evenly over the surface.

6. Bake 33 to 35 minutes. Test for doneness by inserting a tester or toothpick in the center. If a few crumbs adhere to the toothpick or if the toothpick comes out clean, remove the brownies from the oven immediately. With a frosting knife, spread and swirl the softened chocolate chips over the surface to form a glaze. Alternatively, leave the chips to cool without spreading them.

7. Store the brownies tightly covered.

Chocolate Peanut Butter Pizza

This confection is thick, rich, and finger licking good! Because it softens quickly, refrigeration is always a must for leftovers. This pizza can be made round or square.

Pizza

1½ cups semisweet chocolate chips
6 tablespoons (¾ stick) unsalted butter
1 tablespoon light corn syrup

Filling

⅔ cup creamy or smooth peanut butter
3 tablespoons unsalted butter
2 teaspoons milk or cream
½ teaspoon vanilla extract
⅔ cup (or more, if you prefer) confectioners' sugar, sifted if lumpy

1. Line an 8 × 8-inch pan with aluminum foil or plastic wrap (a light greasing helps the wrap adhere to the pan).

2. In a saucepan over low heat, melt the chocolate chips with the butter and corn syrup, stirring to combine and to develop gloss. Alternatively, use the microwave for melting according to the manufacturer's directions.

3. Reserving ¼ cup of the melted chocolate, pour the remainder into the prepared pan, spreading it evenly over the foil from edge to edge. Refrigerate while preparing the filling, although it does not need to be firm to complete the recipe.

4. In a small saucepan over low heat, melt the peanut butter with 3 tablespoons butter and 1 teaspoon milk. Stir to combine.

5. Remove the pan from the heat. Using a wooden spoon, stir in the vanilla. Gradually beat in the confectioners' sugar. Use additional milk or cream if necessary to obtain a filling that's easily spread. (I usually use the specified 2 teaspoons of milk but it depends on how thick your peanut butter is.)

6. Drop the filling mixture by heaping tablespoonfuls over the chocolate. Using a spatula or frosting knife, spread the filling over the chocolate. It doesn't matter if some of the chocolate shows through.

7. Reheat the remaining chocolate, if necessary, stirring to develop a gloss. Spread over the peanut butter. Drag the tines of a fork through the chocolate, creating wavy patterns. Cover with plastic wrap and refrigerate until firm.

YIELD: 12 large or 16 medium bars

DOLORES KOSTELNI

Chocolate Chip Chocolate Drops

These lumpy, bumpy, chewy cookies will satisfy your every chocolate craving.

¾ cup all-purpose flour
2 tablespoons unsweetened baking cocoa
⅛ teaspoon baking soda
Pinch of salt
4 tablespoons (½ stick) unsalted butter, softened
½ cup firmly packed light brown sugar
1 teaspoon vanilla extract
1 large egg white
1 cup semisweet chocolate chips

1. With the rack in the highest position, preheat the oven to 375°F. Prepare a cookie sheet by lining it with aluminum foil. Gloss the foil with baking spray. Using a paper towel, rub the foam over the foil until it is evenly distributed and the surface is glossy.

2. Combine the flour, cocoa, baking soda, and salt and set aside.

3. With the mixer on low speed, beat the butter, brown sugar, vanilla, and egg white until combined. Increase the speed to high and cream the ingredients until light and fluffy.

4. Using a wooden spoon or dinner fork, combine the dry ingredients with the creamed mixture until smooth. The mixture may appear dry, but it will come together in a creamy mass as you stir. Stir in the chocolate chips.

5. Drop by heaping tablespoonfuls in mounds 2 inches apart onto the prepared pan.

6. Bake 5 minutes. Reverse the pan so the back is in the front and bake 4 to 5 minutes longer. The cookies will be set only around the edges and very soft toward the centers. They will continue baking as they cool on the pan.

7. Cool the cookies in the pan on a wire rack for 5 minutes. Carefully remove the cookies to a wire rack for complete cooling.

8. Store any extra cookies in a tightly sealed container.

YIELD: ***a baker's dozen***

6

Special Times, Special Cookies

*T*hink of autumn's falling leaves and pumpkin comes to mind. At Christmas, decorated cutout cookies and spicy little snowballs tease the palate. Fragrant and special, these cookies fill your home with love and sharing, the holiday go-togethers.

This chapter embraces favorite seasonal ingredients and introduces them in exciting new cookie recipes. Gingersnap crumbs enliven the puffy Glazed Pumpkin Pillows while already baked fruitcake forms the basis for unforgettable Fruitcake Déjà Vu Cookies.

Once you and your family have made High Fives and Wooden Spoon Cookies, they'll be favorites for generations. They're the world's best rainy day activities. And they're good to eat, too.

Glazed Pumpkin Pillows
Wooden Spoon Cookies
High Fives
Pfeffernuesse
Christmas Stars
Fruitcake Déjà Vu Cookies
Natalies

Glazed Pumpkin Pillows

A little soft, a little chewy, and full of so much goodness, these could pass as a homey breakfast treat. Either margarine or butter can be used in this recipe. Like most baked goods made with pumpkin, the wonderful spicy flavor develops after sitting for a few hours. Use the same quantity of cooked and mashed sweet potato when pumpkin is unavailable.

¾ cup plus 2 tablespoons and 1 teaspoon finely ground gingersnap crumbs
   (about 12 to 14 small gingersnaps)
⅓ cup all-purpose flour
½ teaspoon baking powder
Pinch of salt
1½ teaspoons pumpkin pie spice
¼ cup raisins
¼ cup finely chopped walnuts, pecans, or hazelnuts
2 tablespoons (¼ stick) unsalted butter or regular corn oil margarine, softened
¼ cup firmly packed light brown sugar
1 large egg white
¼ cup pumpkin puree
1 teaspoon vanilla extract

Glaze

Scant ⅓ cup sifted confectioners' sugar
2 to 3 teaspoons orange juice

1. With the rack in the center position, preheat the oven to 400°F. Prepare a cookie sheet by glossing it with baking spray. Using a paper towel, remove the foam and spread the spray evenly over the pan.

2. Using the food processor, make gingersnap crumbs by processing the cookies in combination with the flour, baking powder, salt, pumpkin pie spice, raisins, and nuts. The cookies should be pulverized to a powder and the raisins coarsely chopped and coated with the mixture. Alternatively, use the blender to pulverize the ingredients in batches. Set aside.

3. In a small bowl, beat the butter, brown sugar, egg white, pumpkin puree, and vanilla until light and creamy. (Don't worry if small flecks of butter speckle the mixture.)

4. Using a wooden spoon or dinner fork, stir in the crumb mixture. The batter will look like wet sand.

5. Drop by 12 rounded, generous tablespoonfuls 2 inches apart onto the prepared pan. Using a fork dipped in water for each cookie, smooth the edges and press the cookies into thick, round patties with a crisscross design on top.

6. Bake 5 minutes. Reverse the pan so the back is in the front and bake 5 minutes longer. The cookies are ready when the surface springs back with a light touch and they are a golden brown. Cool 3 minutes in the pan on a wire rack.

7. Make the glaze by whisking the confectioners' sugar and orange juice together until smooth. Brush each warm cookie with the glaze. Place the cookies on a wire rack for complete cooling.

8. Store the cookies in an airtight container or a well-sealed plastic bag at cool room temperature or in the refrigerator.

Wooden Spoon Cookies

*H*ow you make the craters determines what you'll call these light, colorful delights, favorites to brighten every cookie tray. Whatever the name, thumbprints, jelly craters, or wooden spoon cookies, they have the potential for making the whole gang happy. Use different stuffings—more than one favorite preserve, a few with lemon or orange curd, and a few with mini chocolate chips. When the dough is difficult to shape, dipping your fingers in milk or flour before pinching off pieces makes it easier.

⅔ cup all-purpose flour
¼ teaspoon baking powder
Pinch of salt
4 tablespoons (½ stick) unsalted butter, softened
¼ cup granulated sugar
1 large egg yolk
1 teaspoon vanilla extract
1 tablespoon milk or flour
Favorite preserves, lemon or orange curd, mini chocolate chips
Vanilla sugar, optional (page 89)

1. With the rack in the center position, preheat the oven to 350°F. Line a cookie sheet with aluminum foil.

2. Combine the flour, baking powder, and salt and set aside.

3. Cream the butter with the sugar and egg yolk until light and fluffy. Beat in the vanilla until well combined.

4. Using a wooden spoon or mixer on low speed, stir in the dry ingredients until the mixture is thoroughly combined and forms a ball.

5. Dip your fingers in the milk or flour. Pinch off teaspoon-sized pieces of dough and roll into 12 smooth evenly sized balls. Place on the prepared pan 1 inch apart.

DOLORES KOSTELNI

6. Using the tip of a wooden spoon handle dipped in flour or the small end of a melon ball scoop, make impressions at least halfway into each dough mound.

7. Bake 5 minutes. Remove from the oven. If the craters have shrunk in size, use the rounded side of the ¼ teaspoon to deepen them. Place about a scant ¼ teaspoon of your favorite filling in each crater.

8. Return the cookies to the oven. Bake 5 to 6 minutes longer, or until the edges are barely tan.

9. Cool in the pan on a wire rack for 3 minutes. Remove the cookies to a wire rack for complete cooling.

10. If desired, using a small tea strainer held close to each cookie, sift vanilla sugar on the pastry around the filled center.

11. Store the finished cookies in an airtight container with wax paper between each layer.

✪ ✪ ✪
High Fives

*F*or years, these cookies performed as our family's original finger food. To this day, I use this reliable and tasty recipe whenever I need to make cookies for a crowd. Even though High Fives are an exception to the one-cookie-sheet premise of the book, you would be missing a treasure chest of edible fun and fantasy if I hadn't included them. Using my neighbor Aaron's five-year-old hands as a model, this recipe provides enough dough to make a baker's dozen in pairs of hands and lots of scraps for "jewels" and "rings." Be sure to make a hole in the dough before baking if they're going to be used for hanging decorations.

2⅓ cups all-purpose flour
½ teaspoon baking powder
¼ teaspoon salt
¼ teaspoon nutmeg or cardamom
8 tablespoons (1 stick) unsalted butter or regular corn oil margarine, softened
2 tablespoons solid vegetable shortening
¾ cup granulated sugar
1 large egg
1 teaspoon vanilla extract

Decorating Glaze

1 cup confectioners' sugar, sifted
1 to 2 tablespoons heavy cream
¼ teaspoon vanilla extract
Nonpareils, jimmies, confetti, sprinkles

DOLORES KOSTELNI

1. Combine the flour, baking powder, salt, and nutmeg or cardamom and set aside.

2. In a medium-sized bowl using a handheld mixer, cream the butter or margarine with the shortening until light and well combined. Beat in the sugar, egg, and vanilla until creamy.

3. With the mixer on low speed, gradually mix in the dry ingredients. If the dough becomes too heavy for the mixer, use your hands to knead in the remaining dry ingredients until thoroughly mixed.

4. Divide the dough into 2 smooth disks. Wrap securely in plastic and refrigerate for 1 hour.

5. With the rack in the center position, preheat the oven to 375°F. Line 2 cookie sheets with aluminum foil.

6. Place 1 disk of dough between 2 large sheets of wax paper on a slightly dampened surface. Roll the dough to a ⅛-inch thickness. Remove the top sheet of wax paper.

7. Using a small paring knife or plastic knife dipped in water from time to time (this avoids rough edges), carefully trace around the shape of hands. Trace as many hands as possible on the dough. Carefully lift the dough scraps from around the hands and roll into a ball. Place the prepared cookie sheet over the hands. Holding the hands and cookie sheet together, flip the cookies onto the pan with the wax paper side up. Peel off the wax paper, adjusting any nicks in the cookies. Repeat this process until all the dough has been used.

Or to make "jewels," first gather the dough scraps into a smooth ball. Then place the dough between 2 sheets of wax paper on a slightly dampened surface. Roll the dough to a ⅛-inch thickness. Remove the top sheet of wax paper. Using an assortment of small canape or hors d'oeuvre cutters dipped in flour, cut a variety of shapes for rings, bracelets, charms, and nail adornments. Because "jewels" are small, they bake best in the center of the cookie sheets.

8. Bake 4 minutes. Reverse the pan so the back is in the front and bake 3 minutes more, or until the edges are just beginning to brown.

9. Cool the cookies in the pan on a wire rack for 2 minutes. Lift the foil with cookies from the pan and place on a wire rack for complete cooling.

10. The cookies can be decorated on the foil.

11. In a small bowl, make the glaze by combining the confectioners' sugar, 1 tablespoon cream, and the vanilla. Whisk until it is smooth and thick enough to use as glue and paint. Add more cream by the droplets, if necessary, so that the glaze can be piped through a pastry bag fitted with a # 1 or # 4 writing tip. Make additional glaze for colored baubles and other decorations by adding drops of vegetable dye. Paint the cooled High Fives, or weave lacy gloves and lovely embellishments over the hands and jewels using a glazed-filled pastry bag. Then decorate by attaching "jewels" and your choice of nonpareils, jimmies, confetti, and sprinkles.

12. Store carefully in boxes between layers of wax paper.

YIELD: a baker's dozen of 5-year-old hands plus lots of "jewelry"

Pfeffernuesse

*W*hen *I think of the holidays, these spicy, aromatic, and crunchy "pepper nuts" come to mind. This is a cookie of antiquity, from which all other spice cookies have evolved. The concept of combining black pepper with pungent spices dates back to the Middle Ages.*

¾ **cup all-purpose flour**
¼ **teaspoon baking soda**
¼ **teaspoon each ground cinnamon, cloves, ginger, cardamom, and black pepper**
Pinch of salt
4 **tablespoons (½ stick) unsalted butter or regular corn oil margarine, softened**
¼ **cup tightly packed light brown sugar**
2 **teaspoons dark corn syrup**
1 **teaspoon grated orange zest**
1 **large egg yolk**
2 **tablespoons finely ground blanched almonds**
½ **cup confectioners' sugar, sifted**

1. With the rack in the center position, preheat the oven to 350°F. Line a cookie sheet with aluminum foil.

2. Combine the flour, baking soda, spices, and salt and set aside.

3. In a medium bowl, cream the butter or margarine with the brown sugar, dark corn syrup, orange zest, and egg yolk until fluffy. Add the almonds and beat until they are well blended and invisible.

4. Stir in the dry ingredients. Using your hands, gather the mixture into a ball. Knead several times until smooth.

5. Using a tablespoon as a guide, scoop up the dough and roll between your hands to make 13 evenly sized balls. Arrange 2 inches apart on the cookie sheet.

6. Bake 6 minutes. Reverse the pan so the back is in the front and bake 5 to 6 minutes longer. The balls will have flattened into perfectly round disks and the edges will be firm to the touch.

7. Cool the cookies in the pan on a wire rack until barely warm. Place 2 cookies at a time in a plastic bag with confectioners' sugar. Rotate the bag to coat the cookies heavily, repeating the process until the cookies are snowy. Place the cookies on a wire rack so the sugar sets.

8. Store the cookies in an airtight container.

*YIELD: **a baker's dozen***

Christmas Stars

These spice cookies reach their apogee as aromatic ornaments hung around the house and on the Christmas tree. Cardamom, a member of the ginger family, is an ancient spice from India where its aromatic kernels were called "Seeds of Paradise." Although primarily used as a perfume in ancient Rome and Greece, cardamom was also prescribed to settle an upset stomach. The Scandinavians favor cardamom in pastries and liqueurs while the Indians consider it necessary for properly seasoned curries. The label on the cardamom spice bottle may have the word decorticated listed. This simply means the hull or outer covering has been removed before the flavorful kernels were ground.

1¾ cups all-purpose flour
1 teaspoon ground cinnamon
¼ teaspoon baking soda
¼ teaspoon ground allspice
¼ teaspoon ground mace
¼ teaspoon ground ginger
¼ teaspoon ground cardamom
Pinch of salt
6 tablespoons (¾ stick) unsalted butter
1 cup granulated sugar
¼ cup dark molasses
1 large egg white

Decorator Frosting

1 large egg white
⅛ teaspoon cream of tartar
Pinch of salt
½ to ⅔ cup confectioners' sugar, sifted

1. In a medium bowl, combine 1¼ cups of flour with the cinnamon, baking soda, allspice, mace, ginger, cardamom, and salt.

2. In a small saucepan over low heat, melt the butter with the sugar and dark molasses. While whisking the mixture, raise the heat to medium and bring it to a full boil. Boil the mixture for 1½ minutes, then pour it over the dry ingredients. Using a wooden spoon, beat the dough until the ingredients are combined and uniformly dark. The dough should be smooth.

3. Add the egg white and mix quickly and thoroughly to make a soft dough. Without removing the dough from the bowl, gradually add the remaining flour by the ¼ cupful, kneading it in until the dough cleans the bowl and is no longer sticky. Form the dough into a flat disk. Cover it with plastic wrap and refrigerate it for 1 to 2 hours.

4. With the rack in the center position, preheat the oven to 350°F. Line a cookie sheet with aluminum foil. Coat the foil with nonstick baking spray. Using a paper towel, rub the foam over the foil until it is evenly distributed and the surface is glossy.

5. On a well-floured surface, roll the dough out to a ¼ inch thickness. For each cookie dip a 2½-inch to 3-inch star cookie cutter in flour. Cut out as many stars from the first rolling as possible. Gather up the dough into a smooth ball and repeat the process, cutting out a total of 13 large stars and about a dozen miniature stars. Place the larger stars ½ inch apart on the baking sheet. Place the smaller stars between the larger stars in the center of the pan. Create a falling-stars spray by placing small stars touching each other at the angles, adding additional stars as desired. The cookies will attach to each other as they bake. Using a toothpick, make a hole in the stars for a thread to loop through for hanging. Remember to remove these carefully.

6. Bake 6 minutes. Reverse the pan so the back is in the front and bake 5 to 6 minutes more. The baked cookies will spring back when lightly pressed.

7. Cool the cookies in the pan on a wire rack for 10 minutes. Remove the cookies from the pan to a rack until completely cool. The cookies will firm as they cool.

8. Prepare the frosting by whisking the egg white with the cream of tartar and salt until the mixture is frothy. Gradually add enough confectioners' sugar to make a smooth frosting that's thick enough to pipe through a pastry bag fitted with a small writing tip. Begin by outlining the stars and then finish off with a center decoration. Set the cookies aside for the decorations to firm.

YIELD: *a baker's dozen of larger stars and a galaxy of smaller stars*

◐ ◐ ◐
Fruitcake Déjà Vu Cookies

*T*his could be the ultimate use for leftover fruitcake. The combination of holiday flavors and aromas make these nicely spicy and pleasantly soft cookies a great sweet with hot cocoa during a Twelfth Night tree-burning celebration. Break up the fruitcake and blend it with the spices and other dry ingredients in your food processor. Pulse ON/OFF just long enough to make uniform crumbs that are speckled with larger pieces of glacéed fruits and nuts. The drier the fruitcake, the lumpier the cookie; a flatter cookie results from a moist cake. In any event, these are usually irregularly shaped. For uniform circles, use a cookie cutter to cut the edges away.

1 cup fruitcake crumbs
⅓ cup all-purpose flour
¼ teaspoon baking soda
½ teaspoon ground allspice
¼ teaspoon grated nutmeg
2 tablespoons (¼ stick) unsalted butter, softened
¼ cup packed dark brown sugar
1 large egg yolk
½ teaspoon vanilla extract
Vanilla sugar, optional (page 89)

1. With the rack in the center position, preheat the oven to 375°F. Lightly grease a cookie sheet with solid vegetable shortening.

2. Combine the fruitcake crumbs, flour, baking soda, allspice, and nutmeg and set aside.

3. In a medium bowl, cream the butter, dark brown sugar, egg yolk, and vanilla until light.

4. Using a fork, stir in the fruitcake mixture until well combined.

5. Using the tip of another spoon, push by heaping teaspoonfuls onto the prepared pan.

6. Bake 6 minutes. Reverse the pan so the back is in the front and bake 5 minutes longer. The cookies are done when they are brown and firm to the touch.

7. Cool the cookies in the pan on a wire rack for 2 minutes. Remove the cookies to a wire rack for complete cooling. If desired, shower the cookies with a sifting of vanilla sugar.

8. Store the cookies in an airtight container.

Natalies

Named after my daughter, a sweetheart if there ever was one, this is a cream cheese and butter cookie dough cut into hearts, then decorated with melted chocolate, and finally dressed with a tiny heart "pin."

1¼ **cups all-purpose flour**
¼ **teaspoon salt**
6 **tablespoons (¾ stick) unsalted butter, softened**
1½ **ounces cream cheese, softened (half of a 3-ounce package)**
¼ **cup granulated sugar**
¼ **cup packed light brown sugar**
1 **large egg yolk**
½ **teaspoon vanilla extract**

Chocolate Glaze

½ **cup semisweet chocolate chips**
1 **tablespoon plus 2 teaspoons butter**

1. With the rack in the center position, preheat the oven to 375°F.

2. Combine the flour and salt and set aside.

3. Cream together the butter and cream cheese. Beat in both sugars until well combined and light. Add the egg yolk and vanilla and beat until creamy and light.

4. Using a fork, stir and then hand knead in the flour until the mixture comes together in a ball.

5. Place the dough on a lightly floured work surface. Cover the dough with a large piece of wax paper.

6. Roll out the dough to a ¼-inch thickness. Using a flour-dipped 2½- to 3-inch heart-shaped cutter for each cookie, cut out 12 hearts, using almost all of the dough. There will be enough remaining dough to cut out more than a dozen tiny hearts, using a canapé or hors d'oeuvre cutter. (These extras make nice baker's and helper's rewards.) Place these in the center area; these are small and bake quickly. Place the cookie hearts on a baking sheet with only a little space between each one since these do not spread during baking.

7. Bake 5 minutes. Reverse the pan so the back is in the front and bake 5 minutes longer. The cookies are mostly pale with touches of golden brown around the edges.

8. Cool the cookies in the pan on a wire rack for about 4 minutes. Carefully remove the cookies to a wire rack for complete cooling.

9. In a small pan, make the Chocolate Glaze by melting the chocolate chips with the butter. Stir until smooth and glossy.

10. With a small butter knife or frosting spatula, spread the glaze diagonally on half of each large heart.

11. Carefully attach one small heart to the freshly applied chocolate. Place the cookies on a wire rack until the glaze sets.

12. Store these splendid sweets in a cookie jar with a loose-fitting lid at cool room temperature. (Refrigeration will cause the chocolate to develop a dull, gray "bloom.")

7

● ● ●

Foreign Affairs

Many cookies with international reputations boast lineages dating back to ancient times. Amaretti, the Italian almond macaroons, owe their existence to the Saracen invasions centuries ago. Crescent-shaped walnut cookies from Austria and Hungary provided silent clever communication symbols from the bakery underground about the nearness of the Turkish armies.

Although the original recipes were basic and uncomplicated, they've been refined and simplified over the centuries. The mortar and pestle, effectively used for ages to pulverize seeds and nuts, has given way to the food processor, the magical kitchen machine that reduces whole nuts to a fine powder within moments.

Indeed, cookies with names from faraway places are a mainstay in the coffeehouses and pastry shops around the world. Delicate, sweet Mexican Wedding Cookies have been adopted and adapted by the world as a traditional favorite. At the many konditoreien we visited in Austria, trays of snowy Viennese Crescents were in abundance. In Athens, clove-scented Kourabiethes played a dominant part in the daily dessert ritual. In Budapest and Prague, a dazzling array of buttery nut-encrusted, poppy seed–flecked, and jam-filled rounds, squares, twists, and pockets beckoned.

Wherever the flag of Great Britain flies, tearooms in Hong Kong, Auckland, Rotorua, Sydney, and Melbourne display lavish arrangements of shortbreads and favorite small sweets from the Mother Country. Many are in this chapter for you to make and enjoy.

Positano Amaretti
Italian Pastry Shop Almond Macaroons
Elizabeth's Hungarian Walnut and Sour Cream Cookies
Mexican Wedding Cookies
Greek Almond Cookies (*Kourabiethes*)
Viennese Crescents
Irish Lace
Almond and Hazelnut Biscotti
Christmas Biscotti
Homestyle Chinese Almond Cookies
Florentines
Dried Cranberry Florentines
Dried Cherry Florentines
Lemon Madeleines
Triple Chocolate Madeleines
Spicy Carrot Madeleines
Most Literary Madeleines
New Zealand Madeleines
Anzacs
Australian Melting Moments
Shortbread
Shortbread Fans
Pam's Oatmeal Shortbread
Turtle-Stuffed Oatmeal Shortbread
Cranberry and Nut–Stuffed Oatmeal Shortbread
Rotorua Tearoom Cookies

DOLORES KOSTELNI

❂ ❂ ❂
Positano Amaretti

*T*hese are as special as a cookie gets. These softly chewy, a little bit crunchy macaroons date back to the many types of nut cookies we couldn't get enough of while vactioning in Positano, Italy, years before the seaside town became a tourist haven. Historically, macaroon recipes are centuries old, a remnant of the Saracen invasions. Pignoli come from the cones of a particular pine tree. Because these nuts posess a fragile composition and become rancid easily, store them in a tightly sealed container in the freezer. In keeping with antiquity, some of the nuts are not fully pulverized, which produces an unusual texture. When I serve a buffet dinner, I like to have these as one of the petite finger desserts, with a pot of chocolate fondue on hand for dipping.

1 8-ounce can almond paste
½ cup granulated sugar
Pinch of salt
¾ cup blanched pignoli or slivered almonds
1 large egg white
¼ to ½ teaspoon almond extract

1. With the rack in the center position, preheat the oven to 350°F. Line a cookie sheet with aluminum foil. Coat the foil with baking spray. Using a paper towel, remove the foam and spread the spray evenly over the pan.

2. In the workbowl of a food processor fitted with the steel blade, process the almond paste, sugar, and salt until the ingredients resemble sand.

3. Add ¼ cup pignoli or slivered almonds. Pulse ON/OFF 3 times. Combine the egg white with the almond extract. With the machine running, pour the egg white mixture down the feed tube. The mixture will become uniformly wet. Stop the machine and scrape the mixture away from the sides and up from the bottom.

4. Using a rounded tablespoonful as a guide and with wet fingers dipped in cold water for each cookie, roll the batter into 13 smooth balls. Press one side of each ball in the remaining ½ cup pignoli or almonds. Place 2 inches apart on the prepared pan. With wet fingers, lightly flatten each nut-studded ball.

5. Bake 9 minutes. Reverse the pan so the back is in the front and bake 9 to 10 minutes longer. The cookies will be shiny, with touches of golden brown and slightly crackly tops.

6. Cool in the pan on a wire rack for 1 to 2 minutes but no longer because the cookies may stick. Remove the cookies to a wire rack for complete cooling.

7. Store the finished cookies in an airtight container at cool room temperature.

YIELD: a baker's dozen

Italian Pastry Shop Almond Macaroons

These are similar in flavor and chewy texture to the macaroons found in pastry shops the world over. Find a favorite brand of almond extract—it makes all the difference when making these macaroons.

1 cup slivered blanched almonds
½ cup granulated sugar
1 tablespoon confectioners' sugar, sifted
Pinch of salt
¼ to ½ teaspoon almond extract
1 large egg white

1. With the rack in the center position, preheat the oven to 350°F. Line a cookie sheet with aluminum foil. Coat the foil with baking spray. Using a paper towel, remove the foam and spread the spray evenly over the pan.

2. In the workbowl of a food processor fitted with the metal blade, process the almonds, sugars, and salt until the ingredients resemble sand.

3. Add the almond extract to the egg white. With the machine running, pour the egg white mixture down the feed tube. The mixture will become uniformly wet. Stop the machine and scrape the mixture away from the sides and up from the bottom. Process until the mixture is smooth.

4. Using a rounded teaspoonful as a guide and with fingers dipped in cold water for each cookie, roll the batter into 12 smooth balls. Place on the prepared pan 2 inches apart. These cookies do not spread, but they will puff.

5. Bake 7 minutes. Reverse the pan so the back is in the front and bake 7 to 8 minutes longer. The cookies will be tinged golden brown with slightly crackly tops.

6. Cool in the pan on a wire rack for 4 minutes. Remove the cookies to a wire rack for complete cooling.

7. Store the finished cookies in an airtight container at cool room temperature.

Elizabeth's Hungarian Walnut and Sour Cream Cookies

*T*hese cookies are named after my mother-in-law, a foremost baker who originally hailed from the Buda side of the Danube River. She greatly loved sour cream and walnuts and they found their way into most of her sweets. These featherlight cookie-sized cakes re-create a delicate classic from a past era. Vanilla sugar is the professional baker's secret ingredient.

¾ cup all-purpose flour
¼ teaspoon baking powder
Pinch of salt
Generous pinch of cloves
4 tablespoons (½ stick) unsalted butter, softened
⅓ cup and 1 tablespoon granulated sugar
1 large egg yolk
1 teaspoon grated orange zest
½ teaspoon vanilla extract
3 level tablespoons sour cream
½ cup and 3 tablespoons finely chopped walnuts
Vanilla sugar

1. Combine the flour, baking powder, salt, and cloves and set aside.

2. Cream the butter with ⅓ cup granulated sugar, the egg yolk, orange zest, and vanilla until smooth. Stir in the sour cream.

3. Using a wooden spoon or a fork, stir and fold in the dry ingredients until well combined. While the flour is still visible, add ½ cup finely chopped walnuts and mix thoroughly. The dough may be refrigerated for 1 hour or longer in a covered mixing bowl for easier handling.

4. With the rack in the center position, preheat the oven to 325°F.

5. On wax paper, combine 3 tablespoons finely chopped walnuts with 1 tablespoon granulated sugar.

6. With wet fingers, make 13 equal-sized balls, approximately a rounded tablespoonful each. Roll the balls in the nut and sugar combination to coat completely. Place on the baking sheet about 2 inches apart and gently press down to flatten each cookie into a fat patty.

7. Bake 7 minutes. Reverse the pan so the back is in the front and bake 6 minutes more. The cookies will look puffy and spring back with a gentle touch. A pale golden brown rim will barely show around the edges.

8. Cool the cookies in the pan on a wire rack for 5 minutes. Sift a heavy shower of vanilla sugar over each cookie. Remove the cookies to a wire rack for complete cooling. Before serving, shower again with vanilla sugar.

9. Store these old-world delights in an airtight container.

YIELD: *a baker's dozen*

NOTE: To make vanilla sugar, first split 2 whole vanilla beans and bury them in a canister or a 1-pound box of confectioners' sugar. Let the sugar age for several days before using it. The vanilla beans will infuse the sugar with a delicate fragrance and impart this subtle flavor wherever it is used. Vanilla beans continue to emit their pleasant bouquet for a long time. Remember to replenish the sugar as you use it and you will always have a goodly supply, not only for cookies, but for cakes, and waffles, too.

Mexican Wedding Cookies

Christmas wouldn't be the same without these delightful and delicate cookies. Even today, these are served in Mexico as one of the sweets at the end of a festive dinner. They are a cinch to prepare in the food processor but easily accomplished using standard directions. The foil-lined cookie sheet helps maintain the cookie's classic round shape. However you elect to make them, wait until the cookies are barely warm before coating with confectioners' sugar. If the cookies are too hot, the sugar will yellow and perhaps not even adhere properly.

4 tablespoons (½ stick) unsalted butter, softened
¼ cup and ⅓ cup confectioners' sugar, sifted if necessary
½ teaspoon vanilla extract
½ cup all-purpose flour
½ cup ground pecans

1. With the rack in the center position, preheat the oven to 300°F. Line a cookie sheet with aluminum foil.

2. Cream the butter, ¼ cup confectioners' sugar, and vanilla until light.

3. With a mixer on low speed or with a wooden spoon, stir in the flour and pecans. Continue stirring until the dough comes together in a mass.

4. Using a teaspoon, scoop up spoonfuls of the dough. Roll each piece into a smooth ball. Place on the cookie sheet with space between each one.

5. Bake 8 minutes. Reverse the pan so the back is in the front and bake 7 minutes more. The cookies will have little surface color but there will be a hint of light gold around the bottom edges.

6. Cool in the pan on a wire rack for 2 minutes. Carefully remove the cookies from the pan to a wire rack. When barely warm, place 2 at a time in a plastic bag with ⅓ cup confectioners' sugar and gently rotate to coat the cookies completely. Place on a wire rack until completely cool and the sugar is set.

7. Store in an airtight container.

*YIELD: **a baker's dozen***

FOOD PROCESSOR DIRECTIONS

1. Place the pecans and remaining dry ingredients in the workbowl of a food processor fitted with a metal blade. Process until the nuts are reduced to a powder.

2. Add the butter in tablespoon-sized pieces. Pulse ON/OFF several times to distribute the butter.

3. With the machine running, add the vanilla. Process until the dough cleans the bowl and forms a ball.

4. Proceed as outlined above.

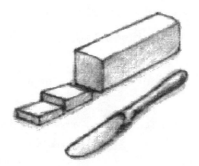

Greek Almond Cookies (Kourabiethes)

This the national Christmas cookie of Greece. The centerpiece clove symbolizes the gifts of the Magi to the Infant Christ in the manger. This recipe is dedicated to our friends in Athens who introduced us to "Greek sweets": Katarina and Nausica with their husbands, the cousins Diamante—sparklingly gracious all.

½ cup plus 1 tablespoon all-purpose flour
¼ teaspoon baking powder
4 tablespoons (½ stick) unsalted butter, softened
¼ cup and ½ cup confectioners' sugar, sifted if necessary
1 large egg yolk
½ teaspoon brandy or vanilla extract
¼ cup ground blanched almonds
13 whole cloves

1. With the rack in the center position, preheat the oven to 300°F. Line a cookie sheet with aluminum foil.

2. Combine the flour and baking powder and set aside.

3. Cream the butter with ¼ cup confectioners' sugar, the egg yolk, and brandy or vanilla until light yellow and fluffy.

4. Stir in the dry ingredients and almonds. Hand knead the dough in the bowl until it is smooth and pliable.

5. Using a teaspoon as a measure, scoop up portions of dough and roll into 13 evenly sized balls. Arrange the balls 2 inches apart on the cookie sheet. Carefully place a whole clove in the center of each ball. Freeze or refrigerate until firm.

6. Bake 8 minutes. Reverse the pan so the back is in the front and bake 7 minutes more. The cookies will be pale on top and lightly golden around the edges; they should not brown.

7. Cool in the pan on a wire rack for 2 minutes. Carefully remove the cookies to a wire rack. When barely warm, place a few at a time in a plastic bag with ½ cup confectioners' sugar. Rotate the bag so the *kourabiethes* are well coated. This will have to be done several times because it's customary for the cookies to be heavily sugared.

8. Store the *kourabiethes* in an airtight container.

*YIELD: **a baker's dozen***

FOOD PROCESSOR DIRECTIONS

1. Place the almonds and remaining dry ingredients in the workbowl of a food processor fitted with a metal blade. Process until the nuts are reduced to a powder.

2. Add the butter in tablespoon-sized pieces. Pulse ON/OFF several times to distribute the butter.

3. With the machine running, add the brandy or vanilla. Process until the dough cleans the workbowl and forms a ball.

4. Proceed as outlined above.

Viennese Crescents

Quick-witted bakers in Old Vienna devised a way of spreading word about advancing Turkish armies by shaping a favorite cookie into the sweet silent code of a crescent—the enemy's symbol. To this day, not only are these the beloved cookie in Vienna, Budapest, and Prague, but they're also one of the world's favorites. Naturally sweet and rich in flavorful oil, walnuts require a deft hand when chopping to a fine consistency. To assure that they don't form a paste, especially in the food processor, add the dry ingredients to the workbowl and pulse ON/OFF until the walnuts are reduced to little dots.

3 tablespoons unsalted butter, softened
3 tablespoons confectioners' sugar, sifted if necessary
¼ teaspoon vanilla extract
⅓ cup plus 1 tablespoon all-purpose flour
⅓ cup finely ground walnuts
Confectioners' sugar, for dusting

1. With the rack in the center position, preheat the oven to 300°F. Line a cookie sheet with aluminum foil.

2. Cream the butter, sugar, and vanilla until light.

3. With a mixer on low speed or a wooden spoon, stir in the flour and walnuts. Continue stirring until the dough comes together in a mass.

4. Using a teaspoon, scoop up 13 evenly sized spoonfuls of the dough. Roll each piece into a smooth 2¼- to 2½-inch stick with slightly tapered ends. Shape into a crescent. Place on the prepared baking sheet with a 1 inch space between each one. Refrigerate or freeze until firm.

5. Bake 7 minutes. Reverse the pan so the back is in the front and bake 5 to 7 minutes more. The cookies will be pale with a hint of tan around the bottom edges.

6. Cool in the pan on a wire rack for 2 minutes. Carefully remove the cookies from the pan to the wire rack. When barely warm, place 2 at a time in a plastic bag with confectioners' sugar and gently rotate to coat the cookies completely. This process may need to be repeated. Place the cookies on a wire rack until completely cool and the sugar is set.

7. Store the crescents in an airtight container.

YIELD: *a baker's dozen*

FOOD PROCESSOR DIRECTIONS

1. Place the walnuts and remaining dry ingredients in the workbowl of a food processor fitted with a metal blade. Process until the nuts are reduced to a powder.

2. Add the butter in tablespoon-sized pieces. Pulse ON/OFF several times to distribute the butter.

3. With the machine running, add the vanilla. Process until the dough cleans the bowl and forms a ball.

4. Proceed as outlined above.

☣ ☣ ☣

Irish Lace

*T*hese cookies are large, delicate, crispy wonders. Alas, humidity is an enemy so make these on dry days. I live in the Shenandoah Valley of Virginia where humidity is invariably high, except during the blessed days of autumn and winter, my seasons for making these. Careful measuring is critical to the success of these cookies: spoon the dry ingredients into the cup and level off without pressing down. Sometimes these cookies run together. If this occurs, as soon as you remove them from the oven, use a large round biscuit cutter to gently and quickly push them back into round shapes.

⅔ **cup quick-cooking or regular oatmeal**
1 tablespoon plus 2 teaspoons all-purpose flour
2 tablespoons (¼ stick) unsalted butter
2 tightly packed tablespoons light brown sugar
2 tablespoons dark or light corn syrup
1 teaspoon heavy cream
¼ teaspoon vanilla extract

1. With the rack in the center position, preheat the oven to 350°F. Prepare the cookie sheet by lining with aluminum foil.

2. Combine the oatmeal and flour and set aside.

3. In a small, heavy saucepan over medium heat, melt the butter with the sugar, corn syrup, and cream. Stir constantly and bring to a rolling boil. The mixture will appear to have lightened and thickened.

4. Remove the pan from the heat. Stir in the vanilla and the combined dry ingredients. Using rounded teaspoonfuls as a guide, drop 13 well-spaced mounds on the prepared pan.

5. Bake 5 minutes. Reduce the temperature to 325°F. Reverse the pan so the back is in the front and bake 5 to 6 minutes longer. The cookies are done when bubbly and a golden color with darker edges.

6. Cool the cookies completely in the pan on a wire rack. Remove the cooled cookies by sliding a spatula underneath them. If some of the cookies are not as crisp as they should be, return them to a 350°F. oven for a few minutes. These cookies burn easily, so watch carefully.

7. These tasty, fragile cookies usually disappear. But in the event a few remain, store in a plastic bag or container with a loose-fitting lid between sheets of wax paper.

YIELD: *a baker's dozen*

Almond and Hazelnut Biscotti

All of a sudden, the entire country has embraced these crunchy, utterly basic, barely sweet, twice-baked Italian cookies. Even in my hometown of Lexington, Virginia, the local coffee shop stacks at least three different varieties in giant jars. They keep beautifully. I grew up knowing there were always some in my Mom's pantry begging to be dunked in cocoa or milk. Although I rarely do it because I'm always short of time, toasting the nuts heightens their flavor and presents the opportunity to rub the hazelnut skins off with a terry towel.

¾ **cup plus 2 tablespoons all-purpose flour**
⅛ **teaspoon baking soda**
¼ **teaspoon salt**
1 egg
⅓ **cup granulated sugar**
2 tablespoons extra light olive oil
1 tablespoon grated orange zest
2 teaspoons vanilla extract
½ **teaspoon orange extract**
⅓ **cup coarsely chopped, unblanched almonds**
⅓ **cup coarsely chopped, unblanched hazelnuts**
1 tablespoon plus 2 teaspoons unsalted butter, melted

1. With the rack in the center position, preheat the oven to 325°F. Line a cookie sheet with aluminum foil. Gloss the foil with baking spray. Using a paper towel, remove the foam and spread the gloss evenly over the foil.

2. Combine ¾ cup flour, the baking soda, and salt and set aside.

3. In a medium bowl using a handheld mixer at high speed, beat the egg, sugar, olive oil, grated orange zest, and vanilla and orange extracts until the mixture is thick and pale, about 2 to 5 minutes, depending on the power of your mixer.

4. Using low speed, incorporate the dry ingredients.

5. Sprinkle the dough with the remaining 2 tablespoons flour. Add the chopped nuts on top of the flour. Knead the nuts and flour into the dough in the bowl until well incorporated and evenly distributed.

6. Scrape the dough into the center of the baking sheet. Using wet hands, shape the dough into a long loaf measuring 11 × 3 inches. The loaf will "grow" a little longer and wider during baking.

7. Bake 25 to 30 minutes, or until a tester inserted in several areas emerges clean. Cool in the pan on a wire rack 10 minutes.

8. Set the oven temperature at 250°F. Using a heavy chef's knife positioned at a 45-degree angle, press the knife into the loaf to cut 1-inch pieces at 1-inch intervals. (Positioning a ruler to one side of the loaf makes cutting even slices easier.)

9. Brush each slice on both sides with the melted butter. Stand the slices on a baking sheet. Bake 10 minutes. Turn off the oven. Leave the biscotti in the cooling oven for 5 minutes.

10. Remove the biscotti from the oven. Cool completely in the pan on a wire rack.

11. Store the biscotti in a plastic bag or an airtight container. These are at their flavorful best a day or two after baking.

YIELD: *a baker's dozen*

Christmas Biscotti

These are perfect treats to have on hand before the serious baking begins. Aromatic, flavorful, and picture-pretty with a speckling of colorful fruits, these also make thoughtful holiday gifts. If you prefer, use chopped dried fruit bits as an alternative to the glacéed fruit and peel. A time-saving hint: Chop the fruits by hand with a heavy, sharp knife. The only fat in these treats comes from the eggs.

1 cup all-purpose flour
½ teaspoon baking powder
¼ teaspoon salt
1 large whole egg
1 large egg yolk
¼ cup granulated sugar
1 teaspoon grated lemon zest
2 teaspoons vanilla extract
3 tablespoons coarsely chopped, mixed glacéed fruit and peel
2 tablespoons coarsely chopped, whole unblanched almonds

1. With the rack in the center position, preheat the oven to 325°F. Line a cookie sheet with aluminum foil. Gloss the foil with baking spray. Using a paper towel, remove the foam and spread the gloss evenly over the foil.

2. Combine the flour, baking powder, and salt and set aside.

3. In a medium bowl using a hand-held mixer on high speed, beat the egg, egg yolk, sugar, lemon zest, and vanilla until the mixture is thick and pale with small bubbles covering the surface, about 2 to 5 minutes, depending on the power of your mixer.

4. Using low speed, beat in the dry ingredients until thoroughly combined.

5. Using a plastic scraper, fold in the chopped glacéed fruits and nuts.

6. Scrape the dough onto the center of the cookie sheet.

7. Using wet hands, shape the dough into a long loaf measuring 10 × 3 inches. The loaf will "grow" longer and wider during baking.

8. Bake 30 minutes or until a tester inserted in several areas emerges clean. Remove the biscotti from the oven. Cool in the pan on a wire rack for 10 minutes.

9. Set the oven temperature at 200°F. Using a heavy chef's knife positioned at a 45-degree angle, press the knife into the loaf to cut off the small end pieces (the chef's reward). Continue pressing the knife into the loaf and cut 12 ½-inch thick pieces.

10. Stand the biscotti on the baking sheet. Bake 10 minutes. Turn off the oven. If you enjoy hard biscotti, leave them in the cooling oven for 10 to 15 minutes. These do not necessarily have to be crunchy hard; if they are lightly toasted with a yielding crumb they are delicious.

11. Remove the biscotti from the oven. Cool completely in the pan on a wire rack.

12. Store biscotti in a plastic bag or an airtight container. These are at their flavorful best a day or two after baking.

YIELD: *one dozen biscotti plus 2 small end pieces*

Homestyle Chinese Almond Cookies

These cookies are unusual, just the way they're supposed to be. Serve them with fresh fruit for dessert after the Chinese dinner you made from beginning to end. Whirl regular granulated sugar in your food processor or blender to make it superfine. Although food historians still don't know exactly where the first almond trees grew, they have established they were grown long before the Christian era in parts of Greece, nearly all of Turkey, and throughout the area we call the Middle East.

¾ **cup all-purpose flour**
¼ **teaspoon salt**
1 large egg yolk, beaten
4 to 5 teaspoons water
¼ **cup plus 1 tablespoon solid vegetable shortening**
⅓ **cup granulated sugar**
1 teaspoon almond extract
13 blanched almond halves (optional)
Several drops red food coloring (optional)

1. With the rack in the center position, preheat the oven to 375°F. Line a cookie sheet with aluminum foil. Gloss with baking spray. Using a paper towel, remove the foam and spread the gloss evenly over the foil.

2. Combine the flour and salt and set aside.

3. Beat the egg yolk with 1 teaspoon water and set aside.

4. Cream the shortening with the sugar. Add 2 teaspoons egg yolk-water mixture, 2 teaspoons water, and almond extract. Continue beating until fluffy.

5. With a fork or your fingers, work in the dry ingredients until the mixture forms a ball and cleans the bowl, using the remaining water by the droplets, if necessary, so the dough holds together and forms a smooth ball.

6. Using generous teaspoonfuls as a guide with your fingers dipped in water, roll into 13 evenly sized balls. Place 2 inches apart on the cookie sheet. Flatten each cookie with the floured bottom of a glass, keeping the shape as perfectly rounded as possible. With a 2½-inch cookie cutter, remove irregular edges, using the scraps for rolling into another cookie.

7. If desired, press an almond half in the center of each cookie and brush with the remaining egg yolk mixture. Alternatively, simulate a Chinese baker's chop, his unique signature. Brush each cookie with the remaining egg yolk mixture. Spread several drops of red food coloring on a saucer. Dip a petite fancy cutter (heart, fish, bird) in the food coloring, shake off the excess, and gently press into the center of the cookie.

8. Bake 5 minutes. Reverse the pan so the back is in the front and bake 4 to 5 minutes more, or until the cookies have light brown bottoms with firm edges and a burnished top surface.

9. Cool in the pan on a wire rack for about 2 minutes. Remove the cookies to a wire rack for complete cooling. They will crisp as they cool.

10. Store these cookies in an airtight container.

YIELD: *a baker's dozen*

❂ ❂ ❂
Florentines

These fragile cookies were created by a true Renaissance cook in fifteenth-century Italy. Although classically made with almonds, honey, and glacéed fruits, I prefer using dark corn syrup and fresh orange zest along with the almonds instead. These cookies are notorious for traveling and meeting each other all over the cookie sheet; however, this version emerges in beautiful rounds that haven't wandered too far.

¾ cup plus 2 tablespoons medium-fine chopped almonds
2 tablespoons all-purpose flour
2 teaspoons orange zest
1 tablespoon plus 2 teaspoons unsalted butter
1 teaspoon granulated sugar
3 tablespoons dark corn syrup (or clover honey)

Chocolate Glaze

⅓ cup semisweet chocolate chips
1 tablespoon butter

1. With the rack positioned in the upper third of the oven, preheat the oven to 350°F. Prepare the cookie sheet by lining with aluminum foil.

2. Chop the almonds in a food processor or blender with the flour and orange zest and set aside.

3. In a heavy, flat-bottomed saucepan over medium heat, melt the butter with the sugar and dark corn syrup. While stirring, bring to a rolling boil. The mixture will appear as if it has thickened and lightened.

4. Remove the mixture from the heat. Quickly stir in the chopped nut mixture and mix to combine thoroughly.

5. Using rounded teaspoonfuls as a guide, make 12 evenly sized mounds. Place 2 inches apart on the prepared pan. With wet fingers or a spoon, press down lightly.

6. Bake 5 minutes. Reverse the pan so the back is in the front and bake 5 to 6 minutes longer. (The cookies will darken more as they cool.)

7. Cool the cookies completely in the pan on a wire rack. They will slide onto a spatula easily when cooled.

8. For the glaze, melt the chocolate chips and butter in a small saucepan over low heat, stirring to smoothness. Cool briefly.

9. With a small frosting spatula or a butter knife, spread the melted chocolate from edge to edge on the underside of each cookie. With the tines of a fork, make a wavy pattern in the chocolate. Place the cookies chocolate side up on a wire rack until the glaze has completely set.

VARIATIONS ON A THEME

Dried Cranberry or Dried Cherry Florentines

1. Reduce the chopped almonds to ⅔ cup.

2. Add 3 tablespoons dried cranberries or dried cherries. Proceed as outlined above.

DOLORES KOSTELNI

Lemon Madeleines

These elegant and sprightly little cakes will quickly become your favorite. An easy way to obtain zest from a lemon is to use a vegetable peeler and slice off thin pieces of the rind, leaving the bitter white pith behind. Use the food processor with the metal blade and whirl the rind with the sugar until tiny yellow dots speckle the sugar.

¾ cup all-purpose flour
¼ teaspoon baking powder
Pinch of salt
5 tablespoons unsalted butter, melted and cooled
2 large eggs plus 1 large yolk
⅓ cup granulated sugar
Zest from 1 small lemon (about ¾ teaspoon)
Few drops of lemon extract or lemon oil

Lemon Glaze

⅓ cup sifted confectioners' sugar
2 to 3 tablespoons fresh lemon juice

1. Gloss the individual madeleine molds with baking spray. Using a paper towel, remove the foam and smear the spray into the ridges. With the rack positioned in the lower third of the oven, preheat the oven to 400°F.

2. Sift the flour, baking powder, and salt and set aside. Melt the butter and set aside to cool.

3. Warm a medium bowl with the eggs and egg yolk over a pan of hot water. (The bowl should not touch the water.) Using a handheld mixer, beat the eggs until frothy. Gradually stream in the sugar, beating at high speed for 2 to 3 minutes or until the mixture is thick and the surface is speckled with small bubbles. Add the zest and lemon extract or oil, beating until the mixture is creamy and thoroughly combined. (Don't worry if the mixture looks slightly curdled.)

4. Using a whisk or scraper, stir and fold the dry ingredients into the creamed mixture. Fold in the butter by dribbling it in little by little. It's important the butter and batter become one without any butter remaining on the bottom of the bowl.

5. Divide the mixture evenly among the prepared madeleine shells, filling each one almost to capacity.

6. Bake 12 to 14 minutes, or until the madeleines spring back when lightly pressed and golden brown edges peek out from the sides.

7. Cool in the pan on a wire rack for 1 minute. Unmold by grasping the pan and rack together and turning the whole upside down so the madeleines unmold. Alternatively, use your fingers to carefully remove each madeleine from the mold. Cool the madeleines completely before glazing.

8. Make the glaze by combining the sifted confectioners' sugar with the lemon juice and mixing until smooth.

9. Brush a thin coating of glaze on each cooled madeleine. After the first glazing, brush each one again. Place the madeleines on a wire rack for the glaze to set.

10. Madeleines are really small cakes, so store them in a plastic bag or covered container at cool room temperature. If you're saving them for a special occasion, madeleines also freeze beautifully.

Triple Chocolate Madeleines

You'll depend on these chubby shell-shaped cookies as the perfect sweet to dress up your dessert tray. Miniature chocolate chips provide the ultimate surprise in these tender and light, chocolate-filled delights.

2 tablespoons unsweetened baking cocoa
½ cup plus 2 teaspoons all-purpose flour
⅛ teaspoon baking soda
Pinch of salt
5 tablespoons unsalted butter, melted and cooled
3 tablespoons semisweet chocolate chips, melted and cooled
1 large egg
1 large egg yolk
1 teaspoon vanilla extract
½ teaspoon water
⅓ cup granulated sugar
¼ cup miniature chocolate chips
Chocolate glaze or ¼ cup vanilla sugar (page 89)

Chocolate Glaze

⅓ cup semisweet chocolate chips
2 tablespoons (¼ stick) butter
3 tablespoons finely chopped nuts, chocolate jimmies, or nonpareils

1. With the rack in the center position, preheat the oven to 400°F. Gloss the individual madeleine molds with baking spray. Using a paper towel, remove the foam and smear the spray into the ridges.

2. Combine the cocoa, flour, baking soda, and salt and set aside.

3. Melt the butter with 3 tablespoons semisweet chocolate chips. Stir until smooth and set aside.

4. Position a medium mixing bowl over a pan of very hot water, without the bowl touching the water. With the mixer on high speed, beat the egg, egg yolk, vanilla, and water until frothy and at least doubled in volume. Gradually stream in the sugar. Continue beating until the mixture is greatly increased in volume and small bubbles speckle the surface.

5. Sift the dry ingredients over the egg mixture. With the mixer on low speed, combine both mixtures.

6. Scrape in the melted butter and chocolate mixture, folding with a scraper until thoroughly combined. It's important the butter and batter become one without any butter remaining on the bottom of the bowl. Fold in the miniature chocolate chips.

7. With a small gravy ladle, spoon the batter into the prepared madeleine shells, filling each one to capacity.

8. Bake 12 minutes. The madeleines should spring back when lightly pressed and a toothpick inserted in several madeleines should emerge clean. If any crumbs adhere, bake a few seconds longer.

9. Cool in the pan on a wire rack for 2 minutes. Unmold by placing the rack over the pan and turning both upside down so that the madeleines come out on the rack.

10. Make the glaze by melting the chocolate chips with the butter. Stir to combine well.

11. Dip the rounded ends of the cooled madeleines in the warm chocolate glaze. Press the glazed end in chopped nuts or other decoration of your choice. Place the madeleines on a wire rack for the chocolate to firm.

12. Or place the madeleines in a plastic bag with the vanilla sugar. Roll the madeleines gently to coat with the sugar.

13. Store like any cake, securely covered in a cool place.

• • •
Spicy Carrot Madeleines

These petite, fanciful shell-shaped cakes are puffed with carrots, currants, nuts, and plenty of fragrant spices. The bread crumbs act as a balance to the high moisture content of the carrots. The easiest way of all to "grate" carrots is in the food processor fitted with the metal blade and using the pulse ON/OFF technique. Vanilla sugar is the baker's secret agent.

¾ cup all-purpose flour
2 teaspoons plain dry bread crumbs
¼ teaspoon baking powder
Pinch of baking soda
Pinch of salt
½ teaspoon cinnamon
¼ teaspoon mace or nutmeg
5 tablespoons unsalted butter, melted and cooled
2 large eggs, beaten
⅓ cup granulated sugar
1 teaspoon vanilla extract
½ cup finely grated carrot, lightly packed (about 1 medium carrot)
3 tablespoons currants
2 tablespoons finely chopped walnuts, pecans, or hazelnuts
¼ cup vanilla sugar (see page 89)

1. Gloss the individual madeleine molds with baking spray. With a paper towel, remove the foam and rub the spray into the ridges. With the rack positioned in the lower third of the oven, preheat oven to 400°F.

2. Combine the flour, bread crumbs, baking powder, baking soda, salt, cinnamon, mace or nutmeg, and set aside. Melt the butter and set aside to cool.

3. Warm a medium bowl with the eggs over a pan of hot water. (The bowl should not touch the water.) Using a handheld mixer, beat the eggs until frothy. Gradually stream in the sugar, beating at high speed for 2 to 3 minutes or until the mixture is thick and the surface is speckled with small bubbles. Gradually add the vanilla, beating until the mixture is thoroughly combined.

4. Pour the dry ingredients on the creamed mixture and place the carrots, currants, and nuts on top of it. Using a fork or scraper, stir and fold both mixtures until thoroughly combined. Using a scraper, fold in the butter by dribbling it in a little at a time. It's important the butter and batter become one without any butter remaining on the bottom of the bowl.

5. Divide the mixture evenly among the prepared madeleine shells, filling each one almost to capacity. This is a thick batter that will distribute itself evenly with baking.

6. Bake 15 to 17 minutes or until the madeleines spring back when gently pressed and golden brown edges peek out from sides.

7. Cool in the mold on a rack for 1 minute. Turn the madeleines out onto a wire rack for complete cooling by holding the rack and pan together so that the pan is upside down and the madeleines unmold. Alternatively, remove each madeleine carefully from the mold with your fingers.

8. Place the cooled madeleines in a plastic bag with the lump-free vanilla sugar.

9. Roll the sugar and cookies together until the cookies are completely coated, adding more sugar as necessary.

10. Serve the madeleines shell side up.

Most Literary Madeleines

These are like the small, shell-shaped cookies of Commercy that French novelist Marcel Proust celebrated in his recollections, A Remembrance of Things Past. *These little cakes are light and tender, though not as humped as the ones Proust loved. Serve these with their beautiful shell sides up, perhaps lightly showered with vanilla sugar or in the New Zealand manner, covered with chocolate or currant jelly and frizzy coconut.*

¾ **cup all-purpose flour**
¼ **teaspoon baking powder**
Pinch of salt
5 tablespoons unsalted butter, melted and cooled
2 large eggs plus 1 large yolk
¼ **cup plus 1 tablespoon granulated sugar**
1 teaspoon vanilla extract

1. With the rack positioned in the lower third of the oven, preheat the oven to 400°F. Gloss a madeleine pan with baking spray. Using a paper towel, smear the spray into the ridges.

2. Sift the flour, baking powder, and salt and set aside. Melt the butter and set aside to cool.

3. Warm a medium bowl with the eggs and egg yolk over a pan of hot water. (The bowl should not touch the water.) Using a handheld mixer, beat the eggs until frothy. Gradually stream in the sugar, beating at high speed for about 2 to 3 minutes or until the mixture is thick and the surface is speckled with small bubbles. Gradually add the vanilla, beating until the mixture is creamy and thoroughly combined.

4. Using a whisk or scraper, stir and fold the dry ingredients into the creamed mixture, a little at a time so no flour ''pills'' develop. Fold in the butter by dribbling it in little by little. It's important the butter and batter become one without any butter remaining on the bottom of the bowl.

5. Divide the mixture evenly among the 12 prepared madeleine shells, filling each one almost to capacity.

6. Bake 12 to 14 minutes or until the madeleines are golden brown and a tester emerges clean.

7. Cool the madeleines in the pan on a wire rack for 1 minute. Carefully remove each madeleine by hand to a wire rack for complete cooling. Alternatively, hold a rack and the pan together so the pan is upside down and the madeleines unmold.

9. Store madeleines, like any small cake, in an airtight container.

VARIATION ON A THEME

New Zealand Madeleines

One afternoon after touring deer farms and trout streams, our bus made a refreshment stop at a small tearoom out in the country. Besides perfectly brewed Earl Grey tea, fancy porcelain dishes with assorted madeleines were presented. Some were dressed like Australian Lamingtons, covered with chocolate and frizzy with coconut. Others wore coats of curly coconut and were still sticky from a dip in currant jelly. In any event, both were marvelous treats.

12 madeleines
½ cup currant jelly, melted, warm
1 cup flaked or grated coconut

1. Coat the madeleines one at a time in the melted jelly.

2. Roll each jelly-coated madeleine in coconut.

3. Place on a wire rack for the coatings to set.

4. Store these unusual sweets between sheets of wax paper in a container with a loose-fitting lid.

Anzacs

These come from my friend Pat Simpson, a third-generation Australian. "Anzac," she writes, "is an acronym and means Australian/New Zealand Army Corps. This has nothing to do with the biscuit—or cookie as Americans say. It is typically Australian and something everyone makes."

Pat uses Lyle's Golden Syrup, a liquid sugar favored by the British, in these cookies. Although this imported syrup is available in many of our supermarkets and in most gourmet shops, dark corn syrup is an acceptable substitute.

Sturdy, plain cookies that travel and pack well, Anzacs are all at once crunchy around the edges and chewy toward the center. The unusual mixing directions make all the difference in producing this distinctively textured cookie.

1 cup quick-cooking (not instant) oatmeal
½ cup all-purpose flour
⅓ cup granulated sugar
Pinch of salt
¼ teaspoon baking soda
4 tablespoons (½ stick) unsalted butter, melted
3 tablespoons dark corn syrup or Lyle's Golden Syrup
1 teaspoon very hot water
½ teaspoon vanilla extract

1. With the rack in the highest position, preheat the oven to 325°F. Grease a cookie sheet with solid vegetable shortening.

2. In a small bowl with a wooden spoon or fork, combine the oatmeal, flour, sugar, salt, and baking soda.

3. Stir in the melted butter. (It will form clumps wherever it touches.) Combine the syrup, hot water, and vanilla and add all at once to the dry ingredients. Mix with the hands or a fork until everything comes together in a ball.

Cookies by the Dozen   113

4. Using a heaping tablespoonful as a guide, roll the mixture into 12 balls and place them 2 inches apart on the prepared sheet. Gently press each ball down to make a fat patty.

5. Bake 5 minutes. Reverse the pan so the back is in the front and bake 5 to 6 minutes more. The cookies will appear pale, lightly freckled, and unbaked yet firm around the edges.

6. Cool the cookies in the pan on a wire rack for 5 minutes. Carefully remove the cookies to a wire rack for complete cooling.

7. Keep these wholesome sweets stored in an airtight container.

Australian Melting Moments

"Although these are not typically Australian," writes my dear friend Pat Simpson from Melbourne, "they're very popular and everyone makes them for Christmas. Most often we leave them plain but some of the time we'll ice them with a sheer frosting or sandwich them with melted chocolate." Indeed, the name says it all.

½ **cup plus 2 teaspoons all-purpose flour**
⅓ **cup confectioners' sugar, sifted if lumpy**
2 tablespoons cornstarch, sifted if lumpy
Pinch of salt
5 tablespoons unsalted butter, very soft and in 5 pieces

1. With the rack in the center postion, preheat the oven to 325°F. Using solid vegetable shortening, grease a cookie sheet.

2. In a small mixing bowl, combine the flour, confectioners' sugar, cornstarch, and salt.

3. Distribute the butter over the dry ingredients. With a pastry blender or fork, cut in the butter (as if making pastry) until it resembles fine meal.

4. With the fingers, continue to blend the fat and dry ingredients until the mixture comes together and cleans the bowl. The dough is soft and easy to shape.

5. Using a heaping measuring teaspoonful as a guide, roll pieces of dough into 13 uniformly sized balls. Place 2 inches apart on the cookie sheet.

6. Using a decorative ceramic stamp or fork, gently press each ball into a 1½-inch circle. Alternatively, the grids of a handheld potato masher make a distinctive pattern, too.

7. Bake 7 minutes. Reverse the pan so the front is in the back and bake 7 minutes more.

8. Cool the cookies in the pan on a wire rack for 4 minutes. Remove the cookies to a wire rack for complete cooling.

9. Store the cookies in an airtight container.

YIELD: *a baker's dozen*

✦ ✦ ✦
Shortbread

*Y*ou have a great deal of latitude with this dough, which is buttery, a little crumbly, and not too sweet, just like the authentic delight you remember from that trip to Britain. It can be cut into various shapes for different occasions: Roll small amounts into balls and flatten with a decorative ceramic stamp. Or cut out hearts and bells to celebrate a wedding shower. For making triangles or fans, which may be the oldest shape of all, follow the instructions in step 4 for patting out the dough but do it on the baking sheet. Score the top into wedges, then bake the circle intact. Press the dough into a 7-inch fluted tart pan with a removable bottom, and a pretty, perfectly round shortbread circle with scored triangles emerges. Unbleached flour produces a wonderfully crunchy short texture that's long on buttery flavor.

1 cup plus 1 tablespoon unbleached all-purpose flour
3 tablespoons cornstarch, sifted if lumpy
¼ teaspoon salt
8 tablespoons (1 stick) unsalted butter, softened
1 teaspoon vanilla extract
⅓ cup plus 1 tablespoon granulated sugar

1. With the rack in the center position, preheat the oven to 325°F. Line a cookie sheet with aluminum foil.

2. Combine the flour, cornstarch, and salt and set aside.

3. In a medium mixer bowl, cream the butter with the vanilla until light. With the mixer on low speed, gradually beat in the sugar by tablespoonfuls, not adding another until the previous one has been completely absorbed.

4. With the mixer on low speed, work the dry ingredients into the creamed mixture a little at a time. Knead in the bowl by hand until the dough is smooth.

DOLORES KOSTELNI

5. On a lightly floured work surface, pat the dough into a ½-inch-thick circle. Using a 1¾-inch floured cutter, cut the dough into rounds. Carefully place the rounds on the cookie sheet. Gather up the scraps and continue to cut dough rounds until all the dough is used.

6. Bake the rounds 20 to 25 minutes, or until lightly golden.

7. Cool 4 minutes in the pan on a wire rack. Remove the cookies to a wire rack for complete cooling.

8. Store the shortbread in an airtight container.

YIELD: *a baker's dozen*

VARIATION ON A THEME

Shortbread Fans

1. Proceed with the recipe through step 3.

2. Press the dough into an 8-inch round cake pan or a 7-inch tart pan with a removable bottom or a free-form 8-inch circle on an aluminum foil–lined cookie sheet.

3. With a sharp knife, score the surface, about ¼ inch down, into 8 wedges. Flute the edges as if for piecrust. Prick generously with a fork and sprinkle with 1 tablespoon of sugar.

4. Bake 35 to 45 minutes, or until lightly golden. (An 8-inch round cake pan requires about 40 minutes; a tart pan with a removable bottom may take the full 45 minutes; a free-form circle needs 35 minutes.)

5. Cool 10 minutes in the pan on a wire rack before cutting completely through into wedges.

YIELD: *8 shortbread fans*

Pam's Oatmeal Shortbread

Although ancient Romans planted oats in Scotland during one of their forays to the British Isles, it took a Scottish sweet tooth to create comforting shortbread from it. Crunchy, slightly chewy, and wholesome, it's as welcome a treat at breakfast as it is with afternoon tea. This is a favorite recipe from my friend Pam, who was born, bred, and married in Great Britain, enjoyed living in New Zealand, and is now having the time of her life in Belgium.

1½ cups quick-cooking oatmeal
1 cup all-purpose flour
1 cup packed light brown sugar
¼ teaspoon salt
¼ teaspoon baking soda
8 tablespoons (1 stick) unsalted butter, melted and cooled

1. With the rack in the center position, preheat the oven to 350°F. Lightly gloss an 8 × 8-inch pan with baking spray. Using a paper towel, rub the foam evenly over the pan until the foam disappears.

2. In a large bowl using a fork, thoroughly combine the oatmeal, flour, brown sugar, salt, and baking soda.

3. Pour the melted butter over the dry ingredients. Using a fork, thoroughly combine until large crumbs form.

4. Pack the mixture evenly in the prepared pan. Bake 20 to 23 minutes. The shorter baking time produces a chewy shortbread while a longer baking period results in crunchy, crisp bars. The shortbread will be golden and a tester inserted at the center will emerge clean.

5. Cool the shortbread in the pan on a wire rack until warm. (The shortbread will firm as it cools.) Cut into bars and cool the bars completely in the pan.

6. Store the shortbread in an airtight container.

YIELD: 12 large or 16 medium bars

Turtle-Stuffed Oatmeal Shortbread

This is a wildly popular bar made everywhere and called everything, including Oatmeal Dream Bars, which they are, except for calorie counters.

Shortbread

1⅓ cups quick-cooking oatmeal
½ cup plus 3 tablespoons all-purpose flour
½ cup packed light brown sugar
¼ teaspoon salt
¼ teaspoon baking soda
6 tablespoons (1 stick) unsalted butter, melted and cooled

Filling

2 tablespoons (¼ stick) unsalted butter
¼ cup packed light brown sugar
2 tablespoons heavy cream
½ teaspoon vanilla extract
1 tablespoon all-purpose flour
⅓ cup chopped pecans
⅓ cup semisweet chocolate chips

1. With the rack in the center position, preheat the oven to 350°F. Lightly gloss an 8 × 8-inch pan with baking spray. Using a paper towel, rub the foam evenly over the pan until the foam disappears.

2. In a large bowl using a fork, thoroughly combine the oatmeal, ½ cup plus 1 tablespoon flour, brown sugar, salt, and baking soda. Pour the melted butter over the dry ingredients. Using a fork, combine the ingredients until large and small crumbs begin to form.

3. Scoop up 1½ cupfuls of the mixture and pack it into the prepared pan. Bake 15 minutes.

4. While the shortbread is baking, add the remaining 2 tablespoons flour to the remaining oatmeal crumbs, mixing with a fork until uniformly sized crumbs form. Prepare the filling. In a small saucepan over moderate heat, melt the butter with the brown sugar and heavy cream. Bring to a boil, constantly stirring. Off the heat, stir in the vanilla and flour until combined and smooth.

5. Pour the warm caramel over the hot shortbread. Strew the pecans and chocolate chips evenly over the caramel. Strew the remaining shortbread mixture evenly over the filling. Bake 20 to 22 minutes, or until the crust is golden.

6. Cool the stuffed shortbread in the pan on a wire rack until warm. Cut into bars. Cool the bars completely before removing from the pan.

7. Store the stuffed shortbread in a well-sealed plastic bag or in an airtight container.

YIELD: *12 large or 16 medium bars*

VARIATION ON A THEME

Cranberry and Nut–Stuffed Oatmeal Shortbread

These are a grand way to use leftover cranberry sauce. If you have less than a cupful of sauce, make up the remainder with either strawberry or raspberry preserves. Any kind of prepared fruit pie filling is great, too; just omit the added sugar.

Shortbread recipe, outlined above

Filling

1 cup whole berry cranberry sauce
2 to 3 tablespoons granulated sugar
1 teaspoon grated orange zest
½ cup chopped walnuts or pecans

1. Preheat the oven and prepare the pan as outlined above.

2. Prepare the shortbread as outlined above.

3. Pack 1½ cupfuls into the prepared pan and bake 15 minutes.

4. While the shortbread is baking, in a small bowl, combine the cranberry sauce with the sugar and zest. Add the chopped nuts and stir thoroughly to combine. Set aside.

5. Using a tablespoon, distribute the cranberry filling over the hot shortbread from edge to edge. Sprinkle the remaining crumbs evenly over the filling.

6. Bake about 35 to 40 minutes, or until the shortbread is golden.

7. Cool the filled shortbread in the pan on a wire rack until warm. Cut into bars. Cool the bars completely before removing from the pan.

8. Store the bars in a well-sealed plastic bag or an airtight container at cool room temperature.

Rotorua Tearoom Cookies

I took an overnight bus trip from Auckland to the resort area of Rotorua during a visit to New Zealand in 1987. We stopped for a midmorning break at a small, plain general store with an adjacent tearoom where they served family-style platefuls of cookies and pots of tea at each table. These unusual, homey cookies, filled with dates, coconut, and crystallized ginger in a soft cream cheese pastry, tantalize with their amazing chewiness. Although the gentleman in charge of the tearoom didn't provide a recipe, he gave me a good idea of how to make them and allowed that in some circles they're called Arabian cookies because of the exotic ingredients. The easiest way to make these is to process the dates, coconut, and ginger in the food processor until they are finely chopped. Then mix in the butter, cream cheese, and vanilla. Finally, add the dry ingredients and pulse until well combined.

⅔ cup all-purpose flour
½ teaspoon baking powder
Pinch of salt
4 tablespoons (½ stick) unsalted butter, softened
1½ ounces cream cheese (half of a 3-ounce package), softened
3 tablespoons granulated sugar
½ teaspoon vanilla extract
⅓ cup whole dates, finely chopped
⅓ cup grated or flaked coconut
2 nickel-sized slices of crystallized ginger, finely chopped
Confectioners' sugar or vanilla sugar (page 89), for dusting

1. With the rack in the center position, preheat the oven to 350°F.

2. Combine the flour, baking powder, and salt and set aside.

3. Cream the butter, cream cheese, and sugar until light and well combined. Beat in the vanilla.

4. Stir in the dry ingredients. Combine the dates, coconut, and ginger with the batter until well combined.

5. Drop by heaping teaspoonfuls 2 inches apart on a baking sheet.

6. Bake 7 minutes. Reverse the pan so the back is in the front and bake 5 to 6 minutes longer, or until lightly browned. Baked cookies will look pale with golden brown flecks.

7. Cool in the pan on a wire rack for 2 minutes. Carefully remove the cookies to a wire rack for complete cooling.

8. Dust with a sifting of confectioners' or vanilla sugar before serving.

9. Store the cookies in an airtight container or well-sealed plastic bag.

*YIELD: **a baker's dozen***

8

Melt-in-Your Mouths

*T*hese are the royalty of the cookie kingdom. Tender, flavorfully rich, and meltingly crunchy, they're a gift to the taste buds. Several served in combination at the end of a dinner or as the sweet with champagne will do you proud.

Fruit Moons are delightful serendipity, a delicious discovery Natalie and I happened upon one afternoon as we made a pie for dinner and talked about the cookies we were going to make for the boys. We wondered what they would be like if the piecrust became big cookies stuffed with chopped fresh fruit. They became one of the most wildly popular cookies we ever made!

Hazelnut Cream Cheese Cookies
Old-Fashioned Crisps
Citrus Wafers
Orange Butter Cookies
Orange Poppy Seed Cookies
Lime Kisses
My Very Best Sugar Cookies
Fruit Moons

Hazelnut Cream Cheese Cookies

This sublime European-style cookie sports a heart of intense chocolate. American hazelnuts come from Oregon, with Barcelona, Ennis, and Casina the most prolific varieties. The hazelnut, also called filbert, dates back to 2838 B.C. when it was primarily used as a medicine, aromatic, and tonic. Its uses are rooted deep in ancient mythology and witchcraft: In some circles it was thought to grow hair on bald heads when combined with suet!

½ cup plus 1 tablespoon all-purpose flour
Pinch of salt
4 tablespoons (½ stick) unsalted butter, softened
1½ ounces cream cheese, softened (half of a 3-ounce package)
½ cup plus 2 tablespoons granulated sugar
¼ teaspoon vanilla extract
¾ cup finely chopped unblanched hazelnuts

Topping

⅓ cup semisweet chocolate chips
2 tablespoons (¼ stick) unsalted butter

1. With the rack in the center position, preheat the oven to 350°F. Prepare a cookie sheet by lining it with aluminum foil.

2. Combine the flour and salt and set aside.

3. Cream 4 tablespoons butter and the cream cheese until fluffy and well combined. Add ½ cup plus 1 tablespoon sugar and vanilla, beating until light and fluffy.

4. Using a wooden spoon or mixer on low speed, stir in the flour until it is thoroughly mixed and the dough forms a ball. Knead in ½ cup hazelnuts.

5. Combine the remaining 1 tablespoon sugar with the remaining ¼ cup hazelnuts.

6. Using rounded teaspoonfuls, roll the dough into 13 evenly sized balls. Coat the balls in the sugar and hazelnut mixture.

7. Place the dough on the prepared cookie sheet and gently flatten into 2-inch circles.

8. Bake 5 minutes. Reverse the pan so the back is in the front and bake 5 to 6 minutes longer, or until the edges are barely golden and the surface is crackled. The cookies will firm as they cool.

9. Cool completely in the pan on a wire rack.

10. Make chocolate centers by melting the chocolate chips with the 2 tablespoons butter and stirring until smooth. Using the ½ teaspoon measuring spoon, place melted chocolate in the center of each cool cookie. Sprinkle the soft chocolate with a little remaining sugar-hazelnut combination. Set the cookies aside for the chocolate to set.

YIELD: *a baker's dozen*

● ● ●

Old-Fashioned Crisps

This large, brown-edged buttery cookie was held in high esteem during days gone by. You'll find these unusually delicious because of the two distinct textures—crisp edges with a softer, slightly chewy center. Take your choice and serve these beautiful rounds plain or sprinkled with cinnamon and sugar or adorned with a perfect nut half or date— whatever strikes your fancy.

¾ **cup unbleached all-purpose flour**
¼ **teaspoon salt**
4 **tablespoons (½ stick) unsalted butter**
½ **cup granulated sugar**
1 **large egg white**
¾ **teaspoon vanilla extract**
12 **pecan or walnut halves or whole dates**

1. Position the rack in the upper third of the oven but not at the highest level. Preheat the oven to 400°F. Generously butter a cookie sheet.

2. Combine the flour with the salt and set aside.

3. In a small bowl, cream the butter with the sugar until light.

4. Beat in the egg white and vanilla.

5. Stir in the flour mixture until well blended.

6. Shape the dough into 12 evenly sized balls and place 2 inches apart on the cookie sheet. Press down lightly to make small patties. At this point, place the nut half or whole date in the center of each cookie.

7. Bake 4 minutes. Reverse the pan so the back is in the front, reduce the oven temperature to 325°F., and bake 4 minutes longer. The cookies will be deep brown around the edges and pale golden in the middle.

8. Cool the cookies in the pan on a wire rack for about 5 minutes. Remove the cookies to a wire rack for complete cooling.

9. Store the crisps in an airtight container.

Citrus Wafers

Orange and lemon zests give sprightly flavor to these picture-pretty cookies. A timesaving hint: Use the vegetable peeler to slice off thin strips of citrus rind or zest—just the colored part with no white pith. Whirl it in the processor or blender with sugar until its dots are barely visible. This technique gives the sugar both flavor and aroma from the oils contained in the citrus skin. Remember when measuring ⅔ cup flour to use the ⅓ measure twice.

⅔ **cup plus 1 tablespoon all-purpose flour**
¼ **teaspoon baking powder**
5 tablespoons unsalted butter, softened
¼ **cup confectioners' sugar, sifted if necessary**
3 tablespoons plus 2 teaspoons granulated sugar
½ **teaspoon lemon zest**
½ **teaspoon orange zest**
¼ **teaspoon lemon or orange extract**
¼ **teaspoon vanilla extract**

1. With the rack in the center position, preheat the oven to 325°F.

2. Combine the flour and baking powder and set aside.

3. Cream the butter with the confectioners' sugar, 3 tablespoons granulated sugar, and zests until light and fluffy. Beat in the extracts.

4. Fold in the flour, mixing and kneading with lightly floured hands until the mixture is well combined and the dough is smooth. (It will retain some stickiness.)

5. Using generous teaspoonfuls of dough as a guide, make 12 uniformly sized balls and roll each one in the remaining sugar. Place them 2 inches apart on a baking sheet. Gently flatten the balls with a fork.

6. Bake 6 minutes. Reverse the pan so the back is in the front.

7. Increase the temperature to 375°F. and bake 5 to 6 minutes longer. The cookies will have pale centers and golden brown rims.

8. Let the cookies cool in the pan on a wire rack for 3 minutes. The cookies will continue to cook on the warm pan and the edges will color slightly more.

9. Carefully remove the cookies to a wire rack for complete cooling.

10. Store these special cookies loosely covered with wax paper in an airtight container.

VARIATIONS ON A THEME

Orange Butter Cookies

Proceed with the ingredients and directions above except:

1. Use 1 teaspoon orange zest only.

2. Use ¼ teaspoon orange extract only.

Orange Poppy Seed Cookies

1. Proceed with the recipe using the seasonings for the Orange Butter cookies.

2. Mix ½ teaspoon poppy seeds with the dry ingredients. Proceed with the directions as outlined above.

☻ ☻ ☻
Lime Kisses

*T*hese small, barely tart and unusually fragrant cookies pair beautifully with afternoon tea. Because limes are thin-skinned, the best way of removing its zest is with a French citrus peeler. It shaves off tiny curls of the flavor-packed rind and leaves behind the bitter white pith. By whirling the lime zest with both sugars in a processor or blender, the green shreds reduce to tiny dots and infuse the combination with its mellow flavor.

1 cup all-purpose flour
¼ teaspoon salt
6 tablespoons (¾ stick) unsalted butter, softened
Zest of 1 lime
¼ cup granulated sugar
6 tablespoons confectioners' sugar, sifted if lumpy
1 teaspoon vanilla extract
1 tablespoon lime juice

1. With the rack in the highest position, preheat the oven to 400°F.

2. Combine the flour and salt and set aside.

3. Cream the butter with the lime zest until light. Gradually add granulated sugar and 3 tablespoons confectioners' sugar. Drizzle in the vanilla and lime juice. The mixture may appear curdled, but continue beating until soft and fluffy.

4. With a small spoon or floured fingers, work the flour mixture into the creamed mixture until it forms a ball. Knead lightly, using small amounts of flour on your fingers until the dough is smooth.

5. Pinch off generous tablespoon-sized pieces of dough and roll into 13 equal-sized balls. Place them 2 inches apart on a cookie sheet. (If the dough is too soft to work with, wrap it in plastic and refrigerate 20 to 30 minutes.)

6. Bake 5 minutes. Reverse the sheet so the back is in the front and bake 5 minutes more, or until the cookies are lightly golden.

7. Cool in the pan on a wire rack for 2 minutes. While warm, shake the cookies in a bag with the remaining 3 tablespoons confectioners' sugar until well coated. Remove the cookies to a wire rack for complete cooling. It may be necessary to coat the cookies again with confectioners' sugar before serving.

8. Store these unusual cookies in an airtight container.

YIELD: **a baker's dozen**

My Very Best Sugar Cookies

Lightly sandy, buttery, and beautifully golden, these perfect rounds are wonderful all the year through. Melt-in-the-mouth, gently sweet delights, they go as well with ice cream and lemonade as they do with espresso or an exotic tea. The combination of baking soda and cream of tartar is an alternate for baking powder.

1 cup plus 2 tablespoons all-purpose flour
Pinch of salt
¼ teaspoon baking soda
¼ teaspoon cream of tartar
4 tablespoons (½ stick) unsalted butter, softened
2 tablespoons plus 2 teaspoons salad oil
¼ cup plus 4 teaspoons granulated sugar
¼ cup packed light brown sugar
1 large egg yolk
½ teaspoon vanilla extract

1. With the rack in the highest position, preheat the oven to 375°F.

2. Combine the flour, salt, baking soda, and cream of tartar and set aside.

3. Cream the butter and oil, gradually adding ¼ cup granulated sugar and the confectioners' sugar and beating until smooth and light.

4. Add the egg yolk and vanilla, beating until pale yellow and fluffy.

5. With a wooden spoon or fork, combine the dry ingredients with the creamed mixture, stirring until the mixture cleans the bowl. The dough will be soft.

6. Using heaping tablespoonfuls of batter as a guide, roll the dough into 13 balls. Roll the balls in the remaining 4 teaspoons sugar and place them 2 inches apart on the cookie sheet.

7. Place a sheet of wax paper over the sugared cookie balls. Using the bottom of a glass, lightly flatten each cookie to the desired thickness. (For chubby cookies, barely press the mounds into 2-inch disks; for thinner cookies, flatten the dough into 2½-inch circles.)

8. Bake 6 minutes. Reverse the pan so the back is in the front and bake 4 to 5 minutes more. The cookies will be uniformly golden and crackly on top.

9. Cool in the pan on a wire rack for 2 to 3 minutes. Remove the cookies to a wire rack for complete cooling.

10. Store the cookies in a tightly sealed container.

YIELD: *a baker's dozen*

Fruit Moons

When Natalie and I made these for the boys as their afterschool treat one day, we had no idea what a tradition they'd become for all of us. Any fresh fruit cut into small pieces is suitable as a filling. Prepared fruit pie fillings do well also. However, don't use preserves. Because they thin with heat, they'll leak out of the pastry sandwich and you'll wind up with an empty moon. Thirteen Fruit Moons line up neatly without the edges touching on a 15½ × 10-inch baking sheet. They make a fantastic buffet and picnic dessert, too.

Pastry

2 cups all-purpose flour
¼ teaspoon salt
12 tablespoons (1½ sticks) unsalted butter, cut in 4 chunks
2 tablespoons solid vegetable shortening
4 to 5 tablespoons orange juice

Filling

2 cups finely chopped apples (2 to 3 medium apples, any type)
1 teaspoon lemon juice
4 tablespoons all-purpose flour
⅓ to ½ cup granulated sugar
½ to ¾ teaspoon ground cinnamon
¼ cup currants
Cold water
Confectioners' sugar, if desired

1. Combine the flour with the salt. Using a fork or pastry blender, cut the butter into the flour until mealy. Add the shortening and cut into the butter and flour until the mixture resembles small and medium field peas.

2. Sprinkle 4 tablespoons orange juice over the flour and fat mixture. Using a fork or your fingertips, distribute the juice to moisten the dry ingredients until it all comes together, cleans the bowl, and forms a ball. It may be necessary to drizzle in the remaining orange juice if the dough is not easily sticking together.

3. Gently knead the pastry 4 to 5 times in the bowl, using a little flour on your fingers to prevent sticking. Divide the dough in half. Gently flatten each half into a thick disk. Cover with plastic wrap and refrigerate while preparing the filling.

4. Prepare the filling by peeling and coring the apples. Chop into small dice. Alternatively, chop in the food processor by pulsing ON/OFF until the desired consistency is reached.

5. Using the same bowl the pastry was prepared in, toss together the apples, lemon juice, flour, sugar, cinnamon, and currants and set aside.

6. Prepare a cookie sheet by lining it with aluminum foil.

7. On a lightly floured surface, roll out 1 pastry disk at a time to a $\frac{1}{16}$-inch thickness.

8. Using a $3\frac{1}{2}$- to 4-inch Texas-sized bicuit cutter or water glass, cut out as many circles as possible. Place the pastry circles close together on the prepared pan without the edges touching. Using the tines of a fork, prick each circle several times. Continue cutting out circles until there are 13 circles of dough on the baking sheet.

9. Gather the pastry scraps into a smooth ball and flatten into a disk. Wrap and refrigerate. Roll and cut the second disk of dough as described in steps 7 and 8.

10. With the rack positioned on the lowest level, preheat the oven to 425°F.

11. Fill each pastry circle with 2 tablespoons of filling, slightly mounding in the center and leaving a narrow edge.

12. For the top crust, take each circle of dough and prick it generously with a fork. Brush cold water on the edges of each bottom circle just before placing the top crust over the filling. Gently press the pastry together at the edges.

13. Using a fork, press the tines into the dough at the edges to seal the top and bottom crusts together. Continue doing this until 13 Fruit Moons have been constructed. (Fruit Moons may be refrigerated or frozen on the cookie sheet at this point, if desired.) Use the small amount of remaining dough for cutting out additional petite heart or star shapes to decorate each Fruit Moon, attaching them to the pastry by using cold water as "glue."

14. Bake the Fruit Moons 10 minutes. Reduce the oven temperature to 375°F. and bake 20 to 25 minutes longer, or until the crusts are golden.

15. Cool the Fruit Moons in the pan on a wire rack for 15 minutes before showering them with confectioners' sugar. They are delicious served warm from the oven.

16. Store Fruit Moons as you would a pie, wrapped or under a dome. Fruit Moons reheat nicely in a toaster oven.

YIELD: *a baker's dozen*

9

· · ·

Twelve-to-the-Bar

Quickly and easily put together, bar cookies are a kissing cousin of drop cookies and a long lost relative of pies and cakes. They combine the best of all three and are thus the most ingenious, the richest, and the most likely to succeed. Fillings never "run over" and foundations never "fall." Always elegant and sumptuous, a few together on a dessert plate will end the simplest meal on a memorable note. These are a dependable cookie for mailing, too, because appearances remain intact during the travails of transit.

Nutty Dollies
Congoes
Lemon Crowned Shortbread
Mazureks
Tearoom Bars
Nanaimo Bars
Key Lime Crowned Shortbread
Toscas

❂ ❂ ❂
Nutty Dollies

A world of fun awaits you in these easily assembled bars. Let your creativity take over. My version boasts a multitude of tasty layers and a hint of salty flavor in lively contrast to the sweetness.

8 tablespoons (1 stick) unsalted butter, melted
1 cup graham cracker crumbs
1 cup semisweet chocolate chips
½ cup flaked coconut
⅔ cup chopped pecans
1 can sweetened condensed milk
½ cup chocolate sandwich cookie crumbs
½ cup plus 2 tablespoons sliced almonds
6 tablespoons chopped lightly salted cashew nuts

Glaze

⅓ cup semisweet chocolate chips
2 tablespoons (¼ stick) butter

1. With the rack in the center position, preheat the oven to 350°F.

2. Melt the butter in an 8 × 8-inch pan in the preheating oven. Tilt the pan so the butter covers the bottom.

3. Layer the remaining ingredients in the order listed, making sure they are evenly distributed from edge to edge. With your fingers or a spatula, press down on each layer to eliminate air.

4. Bake about 20 to 25 minutes.

DOLORES KOSTELNI

5. Cool completely on a wire rack.

6. Melt the glaze ingredients together and stir to combine. Drizzle over the Nutty Dollies before refrigerating overnight.

7. Cut into bars when cold.

YIELD: *12 large or 16 medium bars*

Congoes

*O*ne *of the success secrets for this lusciously chewy, sweet-tooth indulgence is to stir— only stir—with a wooden spoon.*

¾ cup plus 1 tablespoon all-purpose flour
⅛ teaspoon baking soda
¼ teaspoon salt
6 tablespoons (¾ stick) unsalted butter
¾ cup packed light brown sugar
½ teaspoon vanilla extract
1 teaspoon water
1 large egg
½ cup semisweet chocolate chips

Curlicue Glaze

¼ cup semisweet chocolate chips
2 teaspoons butter

1. With the rack in the center position, preheat the oven to 325°F. Lightly gloss an 8 × 8-inch square pan with baking spray. Using a paper towel, remove the foam and spread the gloss evenly over the pan.

2. Combine the flour, baking soda, and salt and set aside.

3. In a small saucepan over low heat, melt the butter. Remove the pan from the heat and let cool slightly. Stir in the brown sugar. Add the vanilla, water, and egg. Stir until smooth and well mixed.

4. Stir in the dry ingredients. While the flour is still visible, fold in the chocolate chips. (They'll pick up a bit of flour, which will prevent them from sinking to the bottom.) Combine thoroughly.

5. Spread in the prepared pan. Bake 28 to 32 minutes. To test for doneness, insert a toothpick or cake tester in the center. If a few crumbs adhere to the tester, the Congoes are baked. A briefer baking time produces soft, chewy Congoes while a longer time yields crunchy edges with a chewy interior. Remove from the oven immediately and place on a wire rack for cooling.

6. When completely cool, prepare the Curlicue Glaze by melting the chocolate chips and butter together in a small saucepan over low heat or in a microwave according to the manufacturer's directions. Stir until smooth and shiny.

7. Using a dinner fork, drizzle the glaze in looping patterns over the Congoes. Let the chocolate cool and firm before cutting the Congoes into bars.

YIELD: 12 large or 16 medium bars

Lemon Crowned Shortbread

A buttery, *tender base and a sprightly citrus topping make this one of the most popular sweets ever devised.*

Shortbread

1 cup minus 2 tablespoons all-purpose flour
¼ cup confectioners' sugar
Pinch of salt
7 tablespoons butter, softened and cut in 5 pieces

Filling

2 large eggs
¾ cup granulated sugar
½ teaspoon baking powder
½ to 1½ teaspoons lemon zest
2½ tablespoons fresh lemon juice
Pinch of salt
1 tablespoon vanilla sugar (page 89), for dusting

1. With the rack in the center position, preheat the oven to 300°F.

2. Sift the flour, confectioners' sugar, and salt into a bowl.

3. With a fork, blend in the butter until the ingredients are well combined.

4. Pat evenly into an 8 × 8-inch pan.

5. Bake 30 minutes, or until pale golden.

6. While the shortbread crust is baking, beat together until smooth the eggs, granulated sugar, baking powder, lemon zest, lemon juice, and salt.

7. Pour the filling over the baked crust. Return to the oven and bake for 30 to 40 minutes, or until a knife inserted in the center emerges almost clean.

8. Cool in the pan on a rack. Dust with vanilla sugar before and after cutting into bars.

YIELD: *12 large or 16 medium bars*

Mazureks

*T*his fine, gently sweet European pastry reflects old-world influences. During our visit to Vienna, Budapest, and Prague, we saw these buttery cream cheese-and-jam–filled pleasures displayed in the coffee and pastry shops. Should you choose to prepare these with just a filling of preserves—omitting the cream cheese and walnuts—its sublime perfection will thoroughly delight you. In both cases, baking time remains the same.

Pastry

1½ cups all-purpose flour
2 tablespoons cornstarch
13 tablespoons unsalted butter, softened
⅔ cup confectioners' sugar, sifted if lumpy
⅓ cup granulated sugar
1 large egg yolk
1 teaspoon vanilla extract

Filling

3 ounces cream cheese, softened
3 tablespoons granulated sugar
3 tablespoons finely chopped walnuts
⅔ cup favorite preserves, slightly warmed and liquidy
Vanilla sugar (page 89)

1. With the rack in the center position, preheat the oven to 325°F. Lightly gloss an 8 × 8-inch pan with baking spray. Using a paper towel, remove the foam and spread the gloss evenly in the pan.

2. Combine the flour and cornstarch and set aside.

3. In a medium bowl, cream the butter with both sugars. Add the egg yolk and vanilla and beat until light and fluffy.

4. On low speed, gradually add the combined flour and cornstarch. Continue mixing until the dough forms large, buttery-looking crumbs. Remove 1 heaping cupful and set aside. Continue mixing the dough until it comes together in a ball and cleans the bowl.

5. Pat the dough evenly over the bottom of the prepared pan, making certain it is level and without any rim around the edges.

6. In the same bowl, beat the cream cheese with the sugar until smooth. Stir in the nuts. Spread over the pastry base, leaving a ¼-inch space around the edges. Pour the preserves over the cheese and nut filling. Sprinkle the reserved pastry crumbs over the preserves and gently pat the crumbs down. (This will also serve to spread the preserves to the edges.)

7. Bake 50 to 60 minutes, or until beautifully golden.

8. Cool completely in the pan on a wire rack before cutting. Shower generously with vanilla sugar.

9. Store the Mazureks in an airtight container.

YIELD: *12 large or 16 medium bars*

Tearoom Bars

A *rich-as-Croesus, wildly popular, sweet tooth treasure that incorporates a buttery crust with a chewy nut and chocolate chip–studded topping. These are at their flavorful best when aged overnight.*

Crust

3 ounces cream cheese, softened
6 tablespoons (¾ stick) unsalted butter, softened
½ cup confectioners' sugar, sifted if lumpy
1 cup minus 1 tablespoon all-purpose flour

Topping

1 large egg
½ cup granulated sugar
1 tablespoon all-purpose flour
¼ teaspoon baking powder
2 tablespoons (¼ stick) unsalted butter, melted and cooled
2 tablespoons dark corn syrup
1 teaspoon vanilla extract
¾ cup coarsely chopped pecans
½ cup semisweet mini chocolate chips

1. With the rack in the center position, preheat the oven to 300°F.

2. In a medium bowl using a hand mixer, beat the cream cheese and butter with the confectioners' sugar until thoroughly combined and light.

3. On low speed, blend in the flour until large crumbs form. Using your hands, gather the mixture into a ball. Gently knead the dough in the bowl a few times for smoothness.

4. Press the dough into an 8 × 8-inch pan.

5. Bake 30 minutes, or until set.

6. While the crust is baking, prepare the topping using the same bowl. Beat the egg with the sugar, flour, baking powder, melted butter, corn syrup, and vanilla until creamy. Stir in the pecans and mini chocolate chips.

7. Increase the oven temperature to 325°F. Pour the topping evenly over the hot crust, tilting the pan, if necessary, to distribute.

8. Bake 30 minutes, or until a knife inserted in the center emerges with a few streaks of chocolate.

9. Cool completely in the pan on a wire rack before cutting into bars.

10. Store in an airtight container.

YIELD: *12 large or 16 medium bars*

Nanaimo Bars

Great memories of two wonderful trips to Vancouver, British Columbia, accompany me when I make Nanaimo Bars. I had my first incredibly immense pieces at the local farmers' market and every bite was a discovery in riches. The clerk, greatly talkative and most proud of this sweet, filled me in on its history. Named after a city on the island, they're a local creation from the '50s. During the holidays everybody makes their favorite versions— mocha, mint, orange, lemon, black raspberry—with newer renditions created all the time.

Although most recipes contain eggs and require some cooking, my simplified interpretation only needs melted butter. The Canadians usually use a custard powder that is available in their supermarkets. In its place, I've substituted easily obtained and inexpensive instant vanilla pudding mix. Once you've tasted Nanaimo Bars, you'll keep a box of pudding mix on hand just to put these together.

Crust

¾ cup plus 2 tablespoons graham cracker crumbs
3 tablespoons granulated sugar
¼ cup grated or flaked coconut
2 tablespoons plus 2 teaspoons unsweetened baking cocoa
¼ cup finely chopped hazelnuts, walnuts, or pecans
5 tablespoons unsalted butter or regular margarine, melted

Filling

2 tablespoons (¼ stick) very soft unsalted butter or regular margarine
1 tablespoon plus 1 teaspoon milk
1 tablespoon instant vanilla pudding mix
½ teaspoon vanilla extract
¼ teaspoon orange extract
1 cup confectioners' sugar, sifted

Glaze

½ **cup semisweet chocolate chips**
1 tablespoon unsalted butter

1. Using additional unsalted butter or regular margarine, lightly grease an 8 × 8-inch pan.

2. In a medium bowl using a fork, combine the graham cracker crumbs with the sugar, coconut, cocoa, and nuts. Pour the melted butter or margarine over the dry ingredients and mix well. Press the crust mixture firmly and evenly into the prepared pan. Refrigerate until well chilled.

3. In the same bowl, prepare the filling. Whip the butter, milk, pudding mix, vanilla extract, orange extract, and confectioners' sugar with a whisk until smooth. Spread over the chilled crust. Refrigerate until firm and well chilled.

4. In a small, heavy saucepan or in a microwave oven, melt the chocolate chips with the butter, mixing until smooth. Spread over the chilled filling. Using a fork, make wavy lines on the chocolate. Refrigerate until cold and firm, several hours or overnight.

5. These bars require protection, so store them securely wrapped in the refrigerator.

YIELD: *12 large or 16 medium bars*

◢ ◢ ◢

Key Lime Crowned Shortbread

*J*ust suppose Bogey and Baby had these scrumptious treats to nibble on as time went by in Key Largo—what a difference it might have made! Christopher Columbus, the peripatetic explorer and number one gourmet, sparked the first lime crop in Florida with seeds that originated in the region of today's Middle East. Many ancient literary references, most especially Tales From the Arabian Nights, *mention the benefits of ''Egyptian lime.''* True Key limes come from the Florida Keys and are as small as golf balls with a green-speckled yellow skin and pale yellow juice.

Crust

1 cup minus 2 tablespoons all-purpose flour
¼ cup confectioners' sugar, sifted
Pinch of salt
7 tablespoons unsalted butter, softened, cut in 5 pieces, and cooled

Filling

2 large eggs
1 large egg yolk
1 14-ounce can condensed milk
⅓ cup fresh or bottled lime juice
½ to 1½ teaspoons lime zest
Confectioners' sugar, if desired

1. With the rack in the center position, preheat the oven to 300°F. Lightly butter an 8 × 8-inch pan.

2. In a medium bowl, make the crust by combining the flour with the confectioners' sugar and salt. With a fork or your fingertips, work the butter into the dry ingredients until it is crumbly. Press into the prepared pan. Prick generously with a fork. Bake 30 minutes.

3. Make the filling in the same bowl by whisking the eggs and egg yolk until light and frothy. While whisking, slowly stream in the condensed milk, lime juice, and zest. Pour over the hot crust.

4. Bake 33 to 35 minutes, or until a knife inserted near the center emerges clean.

5. Cool in the pan on a wire rack. When completely cool, cover with plastic wrap and refrigerate until chilled. Cut into squares. Sift a heavy shower of confectioners' sugar directly over the cut squares, if desired.

6. For best keeping, store these luscious bars completely covered in the refrigerator.

YIELD: *12 large or 16 medium bars*

● ● ● Toscas

This is a personal version of a favorite sweet that originated from my first trip to Maastricht, Holland, where bakeries beckon on each street and every window display tempts and teases. I remember buying something small and luscious from ten bakeries while I walked around, gawking and nibbling. It was this wonderful combination of crunchy almonds, velvety almond custard, tangy sweet raspberry preserves, and tender sugar cookie, all in one heavenly bar.

Cookie Base

1 cup all-purpose flour
¼ cup confectioners' sugar, sifted
Pinch of salt
8 tablespoons (1 stick) unsalted butter, softened and cut in 5 pieces

Filling

Scant 1 tablespoon all-purpose flour
½ teaspoon baking powder
¾ cup blanched slivered almonds
5 tablespoons granulated sugar
5 tablespoons unsalted butter, softened
1 large egg
½ to 1 teaspoon almond extract
4 tablespoons raspberry or strawberry preserves
¾ cup unblanched sliced almonds

DOLORES KOSTELNI

Chocolate Drizzle

½ cup semisweet chocolate chips
3 tablespoons unsalted butter

1. With the rack in the center position, preheat the oven to 300°F. Lightly butter the sides and bottom of an 8 × 8-inch pan.

2. In a medium bowl using a fork, combine the flour, confectioners' sugar, and salt. Cut the butter into the dry ingredients until the mixture is mealy and resembles field peas. Using floured fingers, press the mixture into the prepared pan. Bake 30 minutes, or until pale golden.

3. Prepare the filling. Using the food processor outfitted with a metal blade, process the flour, baking powder, and slivered almonds to combine ingredients and grind nuts to a powder. With the machine running, add the sugar, butter, egg, and almond extract through the feed tube. Process until the mixture is creamy, scraping the workbowl several times.

4. Moments before the crust is ready, warm the preserves of your choice until liquid. Pour the warmed preserves over the hot crust, spreading it from edge to edge. Spoon blobs of the almond paste mixture over the preserves and spread from edge to edge. (It doesn't matter if some preserves show.) Strew the sliced almonds evenly over the topping, gently pressing in to the surface.

5. Bake 20 to 25 minutes, or until golden and puffy and a knife inserted in the center emerges clean.

6. Cool the Toscas completely in the pan on a wire rack.

7. In a small saucepan over low heat, prepare the Chocolate Drizzle. Melt the chocolate chips with the butter, stirring until smooth and shiny. Drizzle the melted chocolate in a close lacy pattern over the surface.

8. When the chocolate has set, cut into bars. Store them tightly covered in a protected area.

YIELD: *12 large or 16 medium bars*

Bibliography

Bagett, Nancy, *The International Cookie Cookbook*, New York, Stewart Tabori & Chang, 1988.

Beranbaum, Rose Levy, *Rose's Christmas Cookies*, New York, William Morrow and Co., Inc., 1990.

London, Anne, *The American-International Encyclopedia Cookbook*, New York, Thomas Crowell Publishers, 1972.

Olney, Judith, *The Joy of Chocolate*, Barron's, Woodbury, New York, 1982.

Sands, Brinna B., *The King Arthur Flour 200th Anniversary Cookbook*, Vermont, Countryman Press, 1991.

Index

E

Elizabeth's Hungarian Walnut and Sour Cream
   Cookies, 88
English Cookies
   Cranberry and Nut-Stuffed Oatmeal
      Shortbread, 121
   Oatmeal Shortbread, Pam's, 118
   Shortbread, 116; variation, 117
   Turtle-Stuffed Oatmeal Shortbread, 119
equipment for cookies, 4–5
extracts and spices, about, 3

F

fats (shortening), about, 1
Florentines, 103; variations, 104
flour, about, 2
French Cookies
   Lemon Madeleines, 105
   Most Literary Madeleines, 111; variation, 112
   Spicy Carrot Madeleines, 109
   Triple Chocolate Madeleines, 107
fruit. *See* dried fruit
Fruit Moons, 134
Fruitcake Déjà Vu Cookies, 80

G

Glazed Banana Oatmeal Mounds, 22
Glazed Pumpkin Pillows, 70
Golden Hermits, 43
Granola Salted Peanut Cookies, 26
Greek Almond Cookies (*Kourabiethes*), 92

H

Hazelnut and Almond Biscotti, 97
Hazelnut Cream Cheese Cookies, 126
Hermits, Colonial, 20
Hermits, Golden, 43
High Fives (decorated), 74
Holiday Cookies, 70–81. *See also* Christmas
   Cookies; Special Times Cookies
Homestyle Chinese Almond Cookies, 101
Hungarian Walnut and Sour Cream Cookies,
   Elizabeth's, 88

M

Macadamia Nut Chocolate Chip Ecstasies, 11
Macaroons
   Chocolate, 58
   Almond, Italian Pastry Shop, 86
   Positano Amaretti, 85
   Surprise, 17
Madeleines
   Lemon, 105
   Most Literary, 111
   New Zealand, 112
   Spicy Carrot, 109
   Triple Chocolate, 107
Marshmallow, Toasted, Mississippi Mud
   (brownie), 45
Mazureks (cream cheese–and-jam-filled), 142
measuring guidelines, 3–4
Melt-in-Your Mouths, 126–34
   Citrus Wafers, 129; variations, 130
   Fruit Moons, 134
   Hazelnut Cream Cheese Cookies, 126
   Lime Kisses, 131
   Old-Fashioned Crisps, 128
   Sugar Cookies, My Very Best, 132
Melting Moments, Australian, 114
Meringue Cookies. *See* Sweet Nothings
Mexican Wedding Cookies, 90
Mint Chocolate Brownies, 63
Miracles (oatmeal–dried fruit), 16
The Most Chocolate Brownies, 61; variations,
   62–64
Most Literary Madeleines, 111
My Very Best Sugar Cookies, 132

N

Nanaimo Bars (coconut nut), 146
Natalies (cream cheese hearts), 81
New Zealand Madeleines, 112
New Zealand, Rotorua Tearoom Cookies (date
   coconut), 122
Nut Date Chews, 41
Nutty Dollies, 138

Oatmeal
   Banana Mounds, Glazed, 22
   -dried fruit, Miracles, 16
   -nut, Old-Timey Traditional Preachers, 51
   -nut, Preachers Gone Astray, 34
   and Peanut Butter Jamwiches, 14
   Raisin Cookies, World's Best, 12
   -raisin, Cowboy Cookies, 27
   Shortbread, Pam's, 118
   Shortbread, Turtle-Stuffed, 119; Cranberry and
   Nut-Stuffed, 121
Old-Fashioned Crisps, 128
Old-Timey Traditional Preachers (oatmeal-nut),
   51
Orange Butter Cookies, 130
Orange Poppy Seed Cookies, 130

About the Author

DOLORES KOSTELNI is currently the restaurant reviewer for the *Roanoke Times & World-News*, and she writes a weekly column entitled "The Happy Cook" for the *News-Gazette* in Lexington, Virginia. She has been a cooking instructor at Washington and Lee University Alumni College, and for eleven years, she ran her own cooking school. Mrs. Kostelni has received several awards for culinary excellence. She is married with five grown children and lives in Lexington, Virginia. COOKIES BY THE DOZEN is her first book.